LEADING
DATA-INFORMED
CHANGE IN
SCHOOLS

SELENA FISK

Solution Tree | Press
a division of
Solution Tree

American version published in the United States by Solution Tree Press

555 North Morton Street
Bloomington, IN 47404
800.733.6786 (toll free) / 812.336.7700
FAX: 812.336.7790

email: info@SolutionTree.com
SolutionTree.com

Visit **go.SolutionTree.com/leadership** to download the free reproducibles in this book.

Printed in the United States of America

Library of Congress Cataloging-in-Publication Data

Names: Fisk, Selena, author.
Title: Leading data-informed change in schools / Selena Fisk.
Description: Bloomington, IN : Solution Tree Press, 2021. | Includes
  bibliographical references and index.
Identifiers: LCCN 2020047343 (print) | LCCN 2020047344 (ebook) | ISBN
  9781951075934 (paperback) | ISBN 9781951075941 (ebook)
Subjects: LCSH: Educational statistics. | Academic achievement--Data
  processing. | Curriculum planning--Data processing. | School improvement
  programs--Data processing.
Classification: LCC LB2846 .F533 2021 (print) | LCC LB2846 (ebook) | DDC
  371.2/07--dc23
LC record available at https://lccn.loc.gov/2020047343
LC ebook record available at https://lccn.loc.gov/2020047344

Solution Tree
Jeffrey C. Jones, CEO
Edmund M. Ackerman, President

Solution Tree Press
President and Publisher: Douglas M. Rife
Associate Publisher: Sarah Payne-Mills
Art Director: Rian Anderson
Managing Production Editor: Kendra Slayton
Copy Chief: Jessi Finn
Production Editor: Alissa Voss
Content Development Specialist: Amy Rubenstein
Proofreader: Elisabeth Abrams
Text and Cover Designer: Rian Anderson
Editorial Assistants: Sarah Ludwig and Elijah Oates

Leading Data-Informed Change in Schools originally published in Australia by Hawker Brownlow Education

© 2020 by Hawker Brownlow Education

ACKNOWLEDGMENTS

Thanks must first go to the leaders who contributed their wisdom to this resource: Catherine Jackson, Chris Mayes, Wayne Chapman, and Terry O'Connor. Your generosity and insights have undoubtedly made this a better resource for educational leaders. Thank you!

Next, thank you to my tribe of extraordinary humans: Tim, Tash, Jhye, Darcy, Catherine, Mel, Kate, Bec, Nicola, Liane, Lucky, Michael, Emma, Shelley, Vic, Carly, Bron, Stacey, Megs, and Suzanne. Ella and LE probably should get a mention too! I am who I am because of you—thank you for being a part of my tribe.

Thanks to the crew at Hawker Brownlow Education. Mark—you've been inside my head far more than most, and I love that you don't think it's a scary place! Michelle— you have done a brilliant job (again!); thank you! Alicia—I will never forget going with you to see my first book for the first time. Thank you for believing in me and this project! And finally, to Elaine—you saw something in my work and took a leap of faith with me. I owe you so much.

Visit **go.SolutionTree.com/leadership** to download the free reproducibles in this book.

TABLE OF CONTENTS

Reproducibles are in italics.

chapter three

STEP 1: ESTABLISH A DATA (OR PROJECT) TEAM. 45

chapter four

STEP 2: UNDERSTAND THE DATA AND THE DATA COLLECTION METHODS 61

chapter five

STEP 3: SELECT AND COLLECT RELEVANT DATA 77

chapter six

STEP 4: DISPLAY RELEVANT DATA IN AN APPROPRIATE FORMAT. 89

ABOUT THE AUTHOR

Selena Fisk has sixteen years of teaching experience in both state and private schools in Queensland, Australia, as well as in comprehensive schools in South London, England. During this time, she has held a range of leadership roles, including learning area-specific leadership (physical education, mathematics, and science) and whole-school curriculum and pedagogy (in Catholic identity, student data and performance, and leading learning, data, and curriculum change)—all of which have strengthened her passion for viewing students as individuals who need adults to fiercely advocate for them and see what they are capable of.

After three years in the role of head of physical education in South London, where she learned about the power of feedback and transparency of results, Selena returned to Australia and began a doctor of education degree at the Queensland University of Technology.

Following the completion of her doctoral thesis in 2017, Selena started her data consultancy practice, Aasha for Schools. As a speaker and facilitator, Selena works with schools, leaders, and regions to develop data-informed strategies for schools, leadership teams, and teachers. Her goal is to help teachers and school leaders see the inherent good that data can bring as well as the benefits of using data to develop thriving learning communities.

Selena can often be found engaging in philosophical data chats or arguments with people who initially worry that she is reducing students solely to numbers. She has not yet started having data chats with her Staffordshire–toy poodle cross (yes—it's a thing!), Ella, but that's probably not too far off. Selena escapes her data brain by going to the beach, running, playing netball, and doing yoga.

In 2019, Selena published her first book, *Using and Analysing Data in Australian Schools: Why, How and What*. She was also recognized as an ACEL New Voice scholar in educational leadership research.

PREFACE

Throughout the process of writing and publishing my first book, *Using an Analysing Data in Australian Schools: Why, How and What*, I became acutely aware of a number of things that I hadn't anticipated when I first started writing. The first was that, while I attempted to find solutions to the question of how to use data well in schools, I was actually creating more questions than answers. Not only are there thousands of ways in which educators can use and analyze data, but some readers were already in a position where they were comfortable with some data collection and analysis—they just didn't know what to do next. Although there are still many people at the "learning about data" stage, there are many more who have moved along the continuum and want to know how to further develop their analysis and insights as well as lead tangible, data-informed change.

Second, as the first book evolved, I realized that the data landscape in schools was changing. In Australia, the National School Improvement Tool has become an established framework in schools, but more broadly across the world, tremendous attention has been directed to learning about and using data across a range of different professions, including in schools. But little educational research and commentary exist to support educational leaders in tangible ways.

Third, in my consultancy work in schools, I learned that some leaders—even those with the best intentions—employed me to be "the bad guy." In some instances, I was responsible for having the difficult conversations with staff and asking the difficult questions about data because some leaders were not sure how or where to start or how to have those conversations with teachers. Leading data-informed change in schools should never just be about a consultant coming in and doing the heavy lifting.

Finally, since starting my first book in 2017, I have been reminded on countless occasions that the conversation about leading data-informed teams and change must be broader than a discussion of the Australian context, as educators around the world are grappling with similar issues to the teachers whom I initially wrote for.

Through all the discussions I have had as a school data consultant, as well as in my work on *Using and Analysing Data in Australian Schools*, I began to see the need for guidance on methods for identifying strategies for change and how schools should step through the processes of collecting and analyzing data, implementing change, and celebrating improvements. If we are truly ready to develop effective and innovative data-informed learning communities, our middle and senior leaders must have the skills to conduct (positive and negative) data-informed conversations with their staff and employ them frequently.

This book offers middle and senior leaders in schools a road map for leading data-informed teams and communities through data-informed change. While there is much already written about leadership styles, leading change, and the benefits of being data-informed, my experience has shown me that transferring an understanding of educational research and change leadership literature to a data-informed context is not always easy or seamless. While leaders may know some relevant literature and have an understanding of what it means to be data-informed, there are no adequate resources that combine research and experience to support the development of data-informed leadership.

As I discussed in my first book, I inherently believe that data have endless potential in our schools, and that data should always be used to have a positive impact in our learning communities and on our students. I believe that data should always be used to catch students out for the right reasons—to recognize things that we may not have known about them before; to show us areas of strength in students; to help us differentiate and cater better for their needs; and to provide opportunities to celebrate growth and achievement. Data should be used to motivate positive change and growth for all learners in our classrooms as well as support their learning in a way that develops thriving learning communities where students are engaged and motivated and where teachers are inspired by the change they can see themselves leading. Data should never be used to catch teachers out, to hold them accountable, or to scare them into action.

I also believe it is necessary for teachers and leaders to be able to articulate their views on, and assumptions of, data to others. If we, as leaders, are not able to clearly state our views on any element of our organization (including data), there is a good chance our teachers will not be able to articulate theirs either. For this reason, and for true transparency, my position on the use of data in schools is as follows.

- Data provide us with information about student potential (which can sometimes be different from what we thought).

- Everyone can learn and improve with effort and application.

- Using data can motivate and engage students.

- Data can be inaccurate or may not reflect a student's true ability.

- Data should be used to inform planning, programs, and differentiation.

- Data can surprise us for the right reasons.

- Data should not be used to catch teachers out but to catch students out—whether they are underperforming, flying under the radar, or achieving great results.

As a leader and as an educator, you too need to be able to identify your views on learning and data, so you can articulate these to the teams you lead.

Leading in the data-informed educational climate has its challenges, but it is incalculably worthwhile to embrace the data with both hands and see what it can do for you. I have no doubt that when you approach data-informed leadership with and for the right reasons, you will see real change in your teams, teachers, students, and the learning community as a whole. Data in schools have immense potential when they are used well. I hope this resource supports you in your pursuit of effective and compassionate data-informed school leadership, and in your change and improvement processes. Have fun with it!

INTRODUCTION

> *The world cannot be understood without numbers,*
> *and it cannot be understood with numbers alone. Love*
> *numbers for what they tell you about real lives.*
> —Dr. Hans Rosling

Data are everywhere. On a Monday morning, our phones know we're heading to work and tell us whether the traffic on the journey will be normal or slow. Data collected on our online activity feed into social media algorithms to deliver targeted advertising, suggest friends we might know, or automatically recognize friends and family in photos. Phones and smartwatches track our steps and activity and tell us when we need to get up and move and even when to breathe.

Some people call data the "new oil." It is powering our economy, it is viewed as an asset that requires an asset strategy, and a handful of organizations own significant amounts of it. As reported in the *Economist*, "Data are to this century what oil was to the last one: a driver of growth and change" ("Data Is Giving Rise to a New Economy," 2017). But unlike oil, we don't trade data for money or for resources—putting data to use in our organizations is how we strike it rich.

In 2017, John Kotter reported that humans had generated more data in the last three years than in all of human history. Take a moment to let that sink in. That is tens of thousands of years' worth of data versus just three! Similarly, James Fisher and Josh Good (2019) found that not only do we have more data available to us than ever before; our *daily* data-driven interactions per person are set to increase from 300 in

2017 to 4,785 by 2025. Whether you choose to argue with the accuracy of the statistics and predictions or not, the increase in data is real and affecting every aspect of our world. Data are creating jobs, changing what is important in our organizations, and forcing us to learn new skills. As noted in the *Economist*, "industrial giants such as GE and Siemens now sell themselves as data firms" ("The World's Most Valuable Resource Is No Longer Oil, but Data," 2017).

Despite the massive amounts of data that we have on tap, using data in organizations is not about the volume of data collected but about how the organization uses the data. Organizations that harness the power of data to create insights and drive action have a real competitive advantage. But translating huge amounts of data into insights does not necessarily come easily—hence the development of the field of data analytics and growth of data science, new university degrees in these fields, and the endless number of programs available to display and view data. Data analytics is not a new technology by any measure, but it has changed and increased in recent years and is now growing rapidly. As Tom Pringle (2019), head of technology research at Ovum, states, "analytics is the engine, and data are the fuel."

Although there is no question about the amount of data we are collecting, or the undisputed power of harnessing the insights contained within the data, industry analysts estimate that just over 30 percent of potential users adopt data analytics effectively in their workplace (Fleming, Pringle, Barker, Fisher, & Potter, 2019). When asked to self-report on their data literacy skills, a 2018 Qlik survey found that only about 25 percent of business users felt they were data literate, and this percentage was even lower in millennials. These findings contradict what we might expect about the level of data literacy in business, and in the skills of our youngest staff. So, we should be careful not to confuse being technologically savvy with being data savvy!

Two key barriers that stand in the way of an organization utilizing analytics to its full potential are (1) the access to and the availability of data and (2) employee skill and ability in using technology and analytics (Pringle, 2019). Until data become part of the culture and not the destination (Fleming et al., 2019), these barriers are not likely to be removed.

DATA AND EDUCATION

Schools are microcosms of society, and as a result of the prevalence of data in every other aspect of our lives, data are consuming the field of education. Countries are compared based on how their students perform in international testing; schools are compared using standardized testing and school-leaver data; students are tracked using their individual data and that of their peers; and in some parts of the world, teachers are tracked and monitored (and paid) using data.

Education never used to be like this. The significant paradigm and cultural shifts that have happened in the data space in schools in recent times have largely occurred since the turn of the century. But like in other industries, these changes have accelerated at a remarkable pace in the last decade. As with other industries over the last ten years, international expectations of education have changed, national education policy and framing documents have changed, and now using data is an expectation of teachers and school leaders around the world. Globally, the use of school data and the comparison of school data are strongly linked to school improvement and evaluation (see Schildkamp, Lai, & Earl, 2013; Schildkamp & Poortman, 2015). In this data-driven world, the people investing in our schools want bang for their buck, as "modern societies no longer tolerate putting large amounts of money into an education system that does not deliver on expectations" (Van Damme, 2019).

As well as developing traditional leadership attributes, leaders are now expected and need to develop the skills of measuring progress and achievement; using and analyzing class, cohort, and school data; and sorting through the myriad of data sources available to determine what is important, all while leading their teams to build these same skills and understanding at the same time. This is a huge task. Further, the complexity of expectations around using data in schools is compounded by the expectations and publication of data in local, national, and international media.

The data culture and data expectations in schools put pressure on educational leaders, as no one can lead a data-informed team through effective and long-lasting data-informed change if he or she does not understand the data to begin with. What happens when someone is appointed to a senior leadership role, and he or she isn't completely comfortable with the data? What if a new principal has always worked with people who have done the analysis for her, and now she is in a position where she needs to demonstrate that she understands what is happening with the data? What if a new deputy or assistant principal has never *had* to be the one who used and responded to data—and now he has to lead data-informed change?

Beyond merely an understanding of the data themselves, and to lead data-informed projects effectively and authentically, the leader must also be able to see, understand, and articulate the inherent good that data can bring his or her organization, and the insights that data could offer that the leader may not have had otherwise. Many leaders also do not understand how we have arrived at a place in the educational landscape where school data dominate national headlines, country comparisons, and school improvement efforts. If school leaders do not buy into the data-informed climate to begin with, they are certainly not going to be able to lead others to effectively engage with the data or evaluate the impact that their school is having.

THE PLACE OF EDUCATIONAL EVALUATION

Although some educators might philosophically disagree with the use of quantitative measures in education, fundamentally, data support the process of evaluating the provision of education to ultimately benefit students. The prime objective of educational evaluation in its purest form is actually well intentioned.

Educational evaluation seeks to monitor the quality of teaching, and to facilitate an improvement in pedagogy and learning where it is needed. Essentially, it strives to improve the learning opportunities for students, so that they have access to better opportunities and teaching. On one hand, this is largely why we entered the teaching profession in the first place—to do the best we could for the students we teach, and so that we could have a positive impact on future generations. But educators tend to view school evaluation negatively as a label (and sometimes as an experience). They also sometimes confuse its intended meaning and purpose.

Quintessentially, evaluating and reflecting on practice and impact as an individual teacher have been professional responsibilities for years—they are not a new concept in the field. In fact, in the 1960s, John Dewey (1963) wrote about the need for reflective practice in schools as a way of shaping the future performance of teachers and students. He stated that teachers:

> *Must survey the capacities and needs of the particular set of individuals with whom [they are] dealing and must at the same time arrange the conditions which provide the subject-matter or content for experiences that satisfy these needs and develop these capacities. (p. 58)*

Teachers would not have chosen to be teachers if they did not see reflecting on their impact and trying to do the best job they could do as some of their core responsibilities.

In the current day, key educational researchers—such as John Hattie and Robert Marzano—repeatedly confirm that teachers are the key school-based influence on individual student performance. Therefore, why wouldn't educational evaluation be

pivotal in supporting the review and reflection of the teacher, and to support and maximize student achievement? Perhaps unfortunately, the evaluation that we often see
in the education sector has progressed far beyond the individual teacher reflecting on
his or her own individual performance—it is now dominated by school comparisons,
is sometimes linked to funding, and, in some parts of the world, is linked to whether
teachers actually keep their job.

THE COLLECTIVE RESPONSIBILITY OF EDUCATIONAL EVALUATION

Sir Michael Barber (2005), a former adviser to former prime minister of the United
Kingdom, Tony Blair, states that educational evaluation is more than just the responsibility of individual teachers—it is of the utmost importance that everyone else in the
school community supports teachers to teach great lessons. Barber (2005) says that
leadership teams and governments play a significant role in the impact that a teacher
has, and it is the responsibility of everyone else involved in the school system—principals, administrators, teacher trainers, government, and other stakeholders—to ensure
teachers are provided with the skills, knowledge, resources, support, and motivation
to teach well.

While much negative attention is drawn to the evaluation of education and its
impact on individual teachers, it is a team effort—middle leaders, senior leaders, system leaders, and governments should all be involved. As leaders in schools, we have
an important role to play. We need to support our teachers and be the subject of evaluation at the same time. Today, teachers are their data, and students are a product of
the effectiveness of their teachers, leaders, and the entire system.

Although it is potentially daunting for teachers to consider that we are in an age
of evaluation and comparison, a benefit of educational evaluation is that it can be
the instigator and main driver in the change process for schools. By evaluating and
reflecting on student performance at a class, cohort, school, state, county, or national
level, educators can identify and then rectify issues, ideally leading to school reform
and improvement. In a perfect world, these improvements in pedagogy would lead to
an improvement in educational outcomes for students. Ultimately, students should be
the ones who benefit from the evaluation and the use of data in schools.

A range of writers in the area of educational evaluation has considered the different ways that educators and leaders could employ practical methods of evaluation in
schools to bring about positive changes and improvements. Scheerens (2002) classifies
four evaluation categories that apply to schools.

1. The first category focuses on students as the object of the evaluation, and includes methods such as student monitoring systems; informal observations and assessment performed by teachers; curriculum testing performed by teachers; development of learning portfolios; and standardized testing initiated by local, regional, and national authorities.

2. The second category focuses on teachers as the object of the evaluation. Evaluation in this sense can take the form of informal or formal methods of teacher appraisal, evaluating teachers and ratings of instructional quality performed by students.

3. The third category focuses on the school (or a department within a school) as the object of the evaluation. Methods include school self-evaluations; department self-evaluations; visitation committees where other schools, local government, and external consultants observe the school; accreditation using predetermined criteria; and external school reviews.

4. The final category focuses on the system of schools as the object of the evaluation, and includes national assessments, formal inspections, and educational indicator projects. The methods by which schools could undertake this type of evaluation in their organization include a mixture of qualitative and quantitative methods.

When viewed through a positive, student-centered lens, all of the four preceding evaluation methods are valid and useful in schools.

Evaluation at all levels has a place in education and has some key benefits. School evaluation can help professionalize the education industry by providing additional information to teachers on how they are serving their students. As a result of effective evaluation, the impact that teachers have in their classrooms improves, and confidence in teachers as individuals and in the broader profession increases in the community (Goldrick, 2002). As leaders, we need to understand the role we play in each of these four levels of evaluation, and recognize and value the importance of evaluation and the role of data in this process.

LEADING DATA-INFORMED CHANGE

Whether we like it or not, leading change is a constant in our schools. There is an increasing expectation on school leaders to lead their teams through data-informed change to ultimately improve outcomes for students. But although leaders might understand a change process, excel at the interpersonal skills required to lead teams effectively, or have great knowledge of how to lead data-informed change, it is difficult to implement data-informed leadership and change in schools because the leader and the school require such a broad range of characteristics and processes in order to do this well.

Success in data-informed leadership relies on the leader having some key leadership attributes as well as the courage and discipline to follow a process for implementing the change that has the right amount of pace, intensity, and human factor, all while engaging staff, motivating students, and convincing other stakeholders of the benefits. It is a massive undertaking! It is completely natural that leaders will be better at some of these aspects of data-informed leadership than others. The challenge is in recognizing your skills and identifying the areas of data-informed leadership that you need to work on.

In the next two chapters, I provide an overview of the context around the place in which we find ourselves with data in schools and consider the way in which evaluation has increased in the education sector and, with it, international comparisons, national expectations, and school tracking methods. This informs the subsequent discussion of how teachers view data, the challenges faced when leading data-informed change, and the research that best supports change efforts.

The remainder of this book is dedicated to the ten-step process for leading data-informed change, with each step of the process described in detail as its own chapter. Each chapter is composed of measurable steps for action and examples of steps that leaders should take, as well as a connection to relevant literature and examples of the ways in which each step could work in schools. These chapters conclude with reflection questions for leaders and their teams.

I am a firm believer that data have the potential to be used to help school communities flourish—by informing practice, improving pedagogy, and improving teaching and learning. But unfortunately, some teachers and leaders do not see the inherent good that data can bring and, instead of embracing and using data to thrive, are fearful of them. As leaders, we need to be able to harness the power of data, promote their use, lead data-informed change for the right reasons in our schools, and bring our staff along with us on the change process. Let's jump into the data!

chapter one

THE CONTEXT OF STUDENT DATA IN SCHOOLS

> *If something is urgent and important, it should be measured.*
> *Beware of data that is relevant but inaccurate, or accurate*
> *but irrelevant. Only relevant and accurate data is useful.*
> *—Dr. Hans Rosling*

Globally, there is now a greater emphasis than ever on making schools more transparent and accountable through the rigorous application of standardized or external testing, accountability, and evaluation measures.

> *At every level—from policy makers at the top, to the teacher*
> *in a small village school—education systems are asking for*
> *more, and better, knowledge. This is not a new phenomenon,*
> *but with evidence-informed policy and practice exerting greater*
> *influence over education in recent years, the demand for reliable*
> *knowledge has increased exponentially. (Van Damme, 2019)*

A noticeable way that the focus on data in the field of education has directly affected teachers, leaders, and school communities around the world is through the inclusion of data skills expectations in teacher standards documentation. Teacher standards are usually country specific, and they outline the expectations on teachers and the practices that are deemed to be effective, and direct teachers' attention to best practice. As a result of the perceived importance of data and monitoring, data can be seen in many recently developed teacher standards frameworks around the world.

THE UNITED STATES

In the United States, teacher certification requirements vary from state to state (Ingvarson, Elliott, Kleinhenz, & McKenzie, 2006). But in addition to each state's expectations for teacher registration, the National Board for Professional Teaching Standards (NBPTS, 2019) certifies teachers for the purpose of improving teaching and learning around the country across five core propositions. The first core proposition—teachers are committed to students and their learning—states, "to inform their pedagogical decisions further, educators analyze assessment data as well, considering it alongside input they receive from family members and other adults involved in their students' lives" (NBPTS, 2016, p. 14). Further, core proposition three—teachers are responsible for managing and monitoring student learning—states, "Accomplished teachers analyze data from standardized examinations, and they design their own assessment tools" (NBPTS, 2016, p. 28). It is worth pointing out that although the NBPTS has been in operation since 1987, the National Conference of State Legislatures (2011) reports that less than 3 percent of teachers across the country were NBPTS certified.

CANADA

In Canada—where different provinces have different teacher standards—the *Standards of Practice for the Teaching Profession* from the Ontario College of Teachers (n.d.), the *Teaching Quality Standard Applicable to the Provision of Basic Education in Alberta* (Ministry of Education, 1997), and the *Professional Standards for BC Educators* (British Columbia Teachers' Council, 2019) do not directly refer to the use of data. But the *Nova Scotia Teaching Standards* (Nova Scotia Department of Education and Early Childhood Development, 2018) state that "teachers are knowledgeable and skilled in the use of assessment for and of learning and the use of assessment data to foster student success" and teachers understand "how to evaluate and utilize assessment data from multiple sources" (p. 10).

AUSTRALIA

In Australia, preservice teachers are expected to "demonstrate the capacity to interpret student assessment data" (Australian Institute for Teaching and School Leadership [AITSL], 2011, p. 19), yet the expectations of teachers and leaders in schools go far beyond this relatively low benchmark. The National School Improvement Tool (developed by the Australian Council for Educational Research [ACER], 2016) expects that:

> *A high priority is given to the school-wide analysis and discussion of systematically collected data on student outcomes, including academic, attendance and behavioural outcomes, and student wellbeing. Data analyses consider overall school performance as well as the performances of students from identified priority groups; evidence of improvement/regression over time; performances in comparison with similar schools; and, in the case of data from standardised tests, measures of growth across the years of school. (p. 4)*

Further, the AITSL *Professional Standards for Principals* (2019) expect principals to:

> *Use a range of data management methods and technologies to ensure that the school's resources and staff are efficiently organised and managed to provide an effective and safe learning environment as well as value for money. This includes appropriate delegation of tasks to members of the staff and the monitoring of accountabilities. Principals ensure these accountabilities are met. They seek to build a successful school through effective collaboration with school boards, governing bodies, parents and others. They use a range of technologies effectively and efficiently to manage the school. (p. 18)*

ENGLAND

In England, the teacher standards state that teachers must "use relevant data to monitor progress, set targets, and plan lessons" (United Kingdom Department for Education, 2011, p. 12) and that they should use these standards in conjunction with feedback from annual appraisals and the Office for Standards in Education, Children's Services, and Skills (Ofsted) expectations. The head teacher standards state that head teachers in England should develop excellent pupils and staff. Specifically, they should "establish an educational culture of 'open classrooms' as a basis for sharing best practice within and between schools, drawing on and conducting relevant research and robust data analysis" (United Kingdom Department for Education, 2015, p. 6).

JAPAN AND CHINA

Although Japan has strict regulations on teachers becoming qualified, it does not have teacher standards, and so does not directly reference the need for teachers to use student data. Interestingly, the high expectations of and on teachers are maintained by the fact that only 30 to 40 percent of education graduates are employed as teachers (Call, 2018).

In China, teachers are expected to engage in lifelong learning, and are generally involved in weekly observations of other teachers, research groups, and professional learning. Like Japan, there are no teacher standards as such, but in Shanghai, there are recognized levels of teacher proficiency (novice, intermediate, advanced, and master teacher). Progression through these levels "is not automatic but rather it is bestowed by district leaders for exceptional practice" (Call, 2018, p. 98).

SOUTHEAST ASIA

In Southeast Asia, the Association of Southeast Asian Nations (ASEAN) and East Timor have addressed the challenge of teacher standards by producing one set of standards that aims to improve the performance of teachers in the region (Teachers' Council of Thailand, 2018). The teacher standards expect teachers to "monitor my students' progress and provide appropriate support" and "use results from assessment to improve instruction" (Teachers' Council of Thailand, 2018, p. 11).

Although the preceding examples only compare teacher and senior leader standards in seven nations, these examples do demonstrate that there are expectations on teachers and leaders regarding the use of data as well as significant gaps between what is expected of teachers and leaders in different parts of the world. What is also clear is that senior leaders are expected to understand student and school data as well as the related processes, reflect on and adjust practices and school approaches where necessary, and then lead their teams and their organizations to be data-informed, improving, and flourishing organizations.

INTERNATIONAL TESTING PROGRAMS

While there has always been considerable anecdotal or qualitative data in schools, the emerging priority and evaluation occurring in schools rely on quantitative measures. This is amplified when renowned educators such as Sir Kevan Collins suggest teachers need to take a more medical approach to teaching because some teachers are "essentially allowed to make it up" as they go (Singhal, 2017, para. 2).

As a part of the school evaluation, monitoring, and change processes occurring in schools, quantitative student data now play a key role in schools and systems around the world. The reliance on quantitative school data is particularly evident locally in school systems that include student data as a part of their performance-based pay system for teachers, nationally where schools are compared on their performance in standardized testing, and globally where schools are compared using international comparisons such as the Programme for International Student Assessment (PISA), the Trends in International Mathematics and Science Study (TIMSS), and the Progress in International Reading Literacy Study (PIRLS).

The development and implementation of the PISA, TIMSS, and PIRLS programs have affected the data-informed culture in schools and systems around the world. The Organisation for Economic Co-operation and Development (OECD) has run the PISA assessments since 2000, where they assess a sample of fifteen-year-old students from around the world in reading, mathematics, and science every three years to "gauge how well the students master key subjects in order to be prepared for real-life situations in the adult world" (OECD, 2018, para. 1).

The core purpose of this assessment program is arguably quite genuine. In fact, Andreas Schleicher, the division head and coordinator of the PISA test, speaks quite rationally and passionately about the purpose of the assessments and the limitations and potential of the use of data they generate. In a TED Talk on using PISA data to build better schools, Schleicher (2012) states:

> Knowing what successful systems are doing doesn't yet tell us how to improve. That's also clear, and that's where some of the limits of international comparisons of PISA are. That's where other forms of research need to kick in, and that's also why PISA doesn't venture into telling countries what they should be doing. But its strength lies in telling them what everybody else has been doing. . . . PISA has shown what's possible in education. It has helped countries to see that improvement is possible. It has taken away excuses from those who are complacent. And it has helped countries to set meaningful targets in terms of measurable goals achieved by the world's leaders. If we can help every child, every teacher, every school, every principal, every parent see what improvement is possible, that only the sky is the limit to education improvement, we have laid the foundations for better policies and better lives.

Despite the criticism and skepticism from some in the field of education regarding international testing and comparisons, it is difficult to criticize the authenticity and optimism that Schleicher demonstrates. Not only does he recognize that the data have limits and that they do not tell countries and systems how to improve; he also recognizes the positive impact that data can have when evidence of improvement is shared with the broader community.

The TIMSS and PIRLS assessments are both run by the International Association for the Evaluation of Educational Achievement (IEA). Since 1995, the TIMSS assessment has evaluated grade 4 and grade 8 student ability in science and mathematics every four years. The IEA states that "assessing [grade 4] students can provide an early warning for necessary curricular reforms, and the effectiveness of these reforms can be further monitored at [grade 8]" (IEA, 2019b).

Similarly, the PIRLS assesses grade 4 students' reading comprehension levels every four years. The PIRLS is slightly different from the PISA and TIMSS assessments as it assesses students' home and school experiences in learning to read. Again, if you were to consider the goals and aspirations of PIRLS, the uses and application of the data it generates are seemingly well intentioned. Regarding PIRLS, the IEA (2019a) states that countries use the achievement and questionnaire data to:

- Monitor system-level achievement trends in a global context
- Monitor the impact of new or revised educational policies
- Pinpoint any areas of weakness and stimulate curricular reform
- Improve teaching and learning through research and analysis of PIRLS data
- Conduct related studies, such as monitoring equity or assessing students in additional grades
- Obtain rich questionnaire data about the home and school contexts for teaching and learning reading

Despite these well-intentioned and almost inspirational reasons for collecting worldwide student achievement data, some educators do not agree with the use of these assessments or the data they collect. Some teachers perceive that these international comparisons reduce students to numbers, and they believe that the data are not a true reflection of the impact of the education system. While it is true that these assessments do not measure things such as students' creativity, concern for others, or interpersonal skills, they weren't designed to. These assessments were designed to track the development of literacy and numeracy skills as one measure of the effectiveness of the education system.

Despite the criticism, I believe that all data have a place in supporting staff and students and that assessments such as these make our schools better places. I believe that assessment data provide useful guidance for teachers, school leaders, systems, and governments, because they are definitive, clear, and less subjective than qualitative data. Like Reeves (2004) states, I believe that "the notion of performance data or analysis of student results is not designed to humiliate or accuse anyone; it is to support the professionals to find reasons for poor achievement and identify specific strategies that work" (p. 52).

DATA USE IN SCHOOLS

When it comes to using data in schools, there is an increasing amount of research in the field that indicates the benefits of using quantitative data in schools and systems. In Australia, education assessment consultant Gabrielle Matters (2006) compares the impact of data in schools to geological upheavals, and states that data can surprise, challenge, and "mark our current views as falsely secure and prone to reversal" (p. 7). At other times, data can reaffirm decisions made in the learning process and confirm and cement our opinions about a student's potential. In addition, data can provide evidence for both teachers and students that the learning process is not having the desired effect and needs to be re-evaluated.

Schnellert, Butler, and Higginson's research (2008) found that teachers experienced new insights about students' needs and their own teaching performance from data that were generated and used in their classroom. Teachers in this study reported that viewing the information and quantitative data on their classes gave them the opportunity to make modifications to their teaching practice, and as a result, teachers became more creative in developing activities they felt better suited the needs of the students. The teachers involved in the study found the quantitative data they collected were the most helpful, more so than qualitative information alone. They stated that data-informed inquiry cycles fuel innovation in classrooms, schools, districts, and governments, and when teachers co-construct and interpret student data, it compels them to act as agents of change in their classrooms and schools.

It is important at this stage to point out that I see a clear distinction between being data informed and being data driven—the way in which we use data in our schools should *always* be data informed. When data have the potential to be used poorly—and are sometimes incorrectly associated with accountability, fear, and teacher checking— as leaders, we always need to ensure that data are used in a way that supports learning communities to thrive, rather than survive (see Kotter, 2017).

Being data informed is the "understanding that data will inform rather than drive decision making because there are rational, political, and moral elements in decision making and data is only one important element in the process" (Shen et al., 2012, p. 3). The benefit of being data informed is that it allows us "to attain a deeper level of understanding about the complexities of teaching and learning, and to learn how to maximize educators' efforts to meet students' needs" (Knapp, Swinnerton, Copland, & Monpas-Huber, 2006, p. 2). This means that in schools, and as data-informed leaders, we use data in a way that recognizes and works alongside the context and complexity of our schools and our knowledge of students. Data-informed leaders and teachers do not focus solely on looking at the numbers—data-informed practice must always include our understanding of people, first and foremost.

RESEARCH BY THE BILL AND MELINDA GATES FOUNDATION

In a project undertaken by the Bill and Melinda Gates Foundation in 2015, researchers surveyed more than 4,600 teachers about the use of data in the United States. In the key summary of their findings, the report states:

> *Teachers believe that knowing their students well is fundamental to effective instruction. Data that matter to teachers are much more than just annual test scores. Data that matter include rich information about students' academic, social, behavioral, and cultural experiences that can help strengthen the connection between teachers and students and shape how learning takes place. (Bill and Melinda Gates Foundation, 2015, p. 3)*

While this report discusses *data-driven* teachers rather than my preferred term, *data-informed*, the research had some interesting outcomes. Seventy-eight percent of teachers involved in the study believed that data help confirm how students are performing and show what is possible, and 61 percent of teachers believed that student data improve their effectiveness as a teacher. Further, 69 percent of the teachers believed that data were important in assisting differentiation so that individualized and targeted teaching could occur to improve achievement. These are remarkably positive findings, with significant proportions of the 4,600 teachers indicating that data have the potential to confirm what they know, improve their effectiveness, and assist with differentiation. But in the same research, 67 percent of teachers reported that they were not fully satisfied with the effectiveness of the tools or the data that they had regular access to. The researchers state that teachers:

> *Feel overwhelmed by the volume of data, worry that the data lack the detail required to address the needs of individual students, and believe that the laborious effort required to pull data together for analysis takes time away from teaching and learning. The average teacher works more than 50 hours per week, and the teachers we surveyed acknowledged longstanding tensions between working directly with students and tasks perceived as more administrative in nature. Despite these challenges, when teachers were asked where they want to spend more time in a 2014 survey commissioned by the foundation, in large numbers they said they wanted to focus on activities that support data-driven instruction, such as lesson planning, reviewing student performance, tutoring students, and collaborating with other teachers. (Bill and Melinda Gates Foundation, 2015, p. 8)*

This means that although large numbers of teachers can see the value that data can bring to their classrooms, the tools and strategies that they currently have are not necessarily meeting their needs as best they could, and what teachers do have access to takes a lot of time out of their week.

These findings align with research that found 80 percent of the time taken up in data analysis is in preparation of the data, rather than the analysis and storytelling (Jones & Pickett, 2019). Therefore, a challenge for school leaders is in maximizing what teachers can achieve in the limited time they have to collect, use, and analyze data to ensure they are having the greatest impact possible. Leaders need to actively seek out tools that help to reduce the data preparation time from 80 percent down to something more manageable so that teachers can focus on using data to shift pedagogy and educational outcomes, rather than preparing and manipulating data.

To achieve these aims, schools and systems need to invest in structures and technological tools to support the data-informed culture and processes and ensure that teachers know how to translate the numbers on a computer to actual, tangible change in classrooms. If leaders are able to do this for their teachers, teachers will be able to spend more time creating more personalized and specific learning activities for their students, which will undoubtedly positively impact outcomes and improve the opportunities that each young person has.

CATEGORIES OF DATA USE

As a part of the research in the Bill and Melinda Gates Foundation (2015) report, the researchers stated that teachers fit into one of six categories relating to the way in which they use data. Teachers are (1) data mavens, (2) growth seekers, (3) aspirational users, (4) scorekeepers, (5) perceptives, or (6) traditionalists. The researchers describe these categories as follows.

- Data mavens focus on individualizing learning plans to address the whole student.

- Growth seekers use data to differentiate instruction in the classroom and adapt how they teach.

- Aspirational users believe in using data but often find it overwhelming.

- Scorekeepers rely on assessment data to help prepare students for state tests and other high-stakes assessments.

- Perceptives rely on their own observations of how students are doing to guide instruction.

- Traditionalists focus primarily on grades as a barometer of student progress and an indicator of where to focus their teaching. (Bill and Melinda Gates Foundation, 2015, p. 4)

Unsurprisingly, the researchers found that there are teachers at all six of the proficiency levels in all schools. But quite surprisingly, they found that 48 percent (nearly half of the teachers) fit into the first two categories (data mavens and growth seekers) and are early adopters of data-informed practices. This is an encouraging statistic for data-informed leaders because it shows that much progress has been made to improve the skills and confidence of teachers with data. It is also considerably higher than the reported amount of only just over 30 percent of employees using data analysis effectively in their workplaces, as reported by industry analysts (Fleming et al., 2019).

But above all, the greatest impact on the proportion of teachers in each category was found to be largely influenced by the school environment. Specifically, in technology-forward schools, the "proportion of data mavens is 15 percentage points higher" (Bill and Melinda Gates Foundation, 2015, p. 4). By *technology-forward*, the researchers mean that in those schools, the principals invest in technological infrastructure and training for staff, they provide dedicated time for teachers to work with and make use of the data, the principal is proficient in the technology, and teachers are free to choose the types of technology and tools that they utilize to use and analyze data. So, when the report states that data mavens are 15 percentage points higher in schools that do these things, it provides clear guidance to leaders and systems on what we could be doing to support our teachers to move into these categories.

Other than the classification of teachers, another outcome of the Bill and Melinda Gates Foundation (2015) study is the recommendations on ways in which school and district leaders can support data-informed practice. The researchers state that leaders should be:

- Using the data-driven instructional model to discuss where existing data procedures and tools support—or fail to support—student learning
- Restructuring learning environments to ensure that teachers have access to rich data every day, and recognizing that the depth of data-driven instruction is dependent on the availability of high-quality tools that keep teachers from being overburdened with administrative tasks
- Seeking out and potentially incorporating existing solutions that innovative schools have already developed
- Supporting teachers by investing in the staff, training, dedicated time, and professional development needed to integrate tools and practice
- Engaging teachers in the process of identifying and selecting new tools and strategies
- Accelerating the shift to personalized learning by investing in infrastructure and high-quality tools
- Explaining to parents and community members the value of data-driven instruction and the safeguards in place to protect student information (Bill and Melinda Gates Foundation, 2015, p. 6)

THE CYCLE OF DATA-INFORMED INSTRUCTION

The final point of interest in the Bill and Melinda Gates Foundation (2015) report was the discussion about the cycle that usually defines data-informed instruction. The researchers found for the teachers who were involved in the study, there were common parts of a data-informed instruction cycle that were repeated several times over, either in the teaching period or in the academic year. The goal of the cycle is ultimately to move student achievement along, through a series of four steps: (1) plan and teach, (2) assess, (3) analyze, and (4) pivot.

The first step, plan and teach, is where teachers plan and deliver an activity, lesson, or learning experience to their class. The pedagogical choices made prior to and during this lesson draw on what the teacher has learned about the individual student needs and abilities in previous lessons and assessments.

At some stage during the activity or afterward, the teacher assesses his or her students for the second step. This assessment provides information to the teacher about the depth of understanding of his or her students and may vary from informal, short, formative assessments through to formal, longer, or even summative assessment.

In the analyze step, teachers investigate the data individually and in their teaching teams to identify areas of need. In this step, anecdotal evidence or observations of student learning could be confirmed by the assessment data—such as that students may have reached a level of mastery, or they may require additional teaching. It is also possible at this stage that the data could indicate that students did not understand the concepts as well as the teacher believed.

The fourth step, pivot, is where teachers adjust their approach and pedagogy in follow-up activities or lessons based on the analysis of the data. This might involve reteaching a targeted group of students within the class, or the class as a whole. The cycle then returns to the plan and teach stage, where the data analysis informs the next cycle of teaching, and the cycle begins again.

TYPES OF DATA AVAILABLE IN SCHOOLS

> *Forrester research predicts that data-driven public companies will grow seven times faster than the global GDP, or 27 percent per year. Companies with data at their center will improve, those who don't, won't.*
> —*Tableau Software, 2019*

For the data-informed instruction cycle to be effective, teachers must have a number of things available to them. They must understand how to collect data on their students to begin with. They must be able to collect and analyze the data in a timely fashion so that they can pivot their instruction. They must have the data analysis skills they need to ascertain trends in the data and the possible options for change, and they must be willing and able to repeat this process indefinitely. Bearing in mind that 52 percent of teachers do not fit into the categories of data mavens and growth seekers, school leaders need to do their utmost to provide the conditions required for teachers to improve in their use of data.

But what data do we have in schools exactly? International comparisons, national testing, and learning area results are all obvious sources, but there are many other types of data available in our schools. Victoria Bernhardt is the executive director of Education for the Future, and she has gained worldwide attention for the way in which she works with schools to utilize the power of data. She advocates for the use of multiple data measures to analyze and monitor the performance of a school, rather than a single measure of student achievement. As shown in figure 1.1, Bernhardt (2018) focuses on four broad categories of data: (1) demographics, (2) perceptions, (3) school processes, and (4) student learning. The overlap between two and three categories provides more detailed information about the impact of more than one factor. For example, the overlap of student learning, school processes, and demographics circles tells us about the impact of particular school programs on student learning for different groups of students.

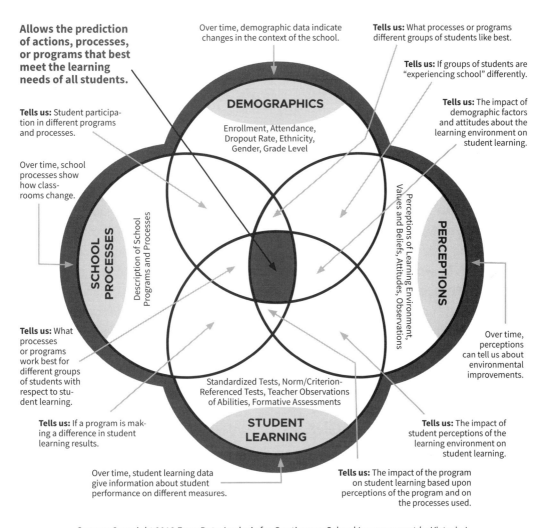

Source: *Copyright 2018 From* Data Analysis for Continuous School Improvement *by Victoria L. Bernhardt. Reproduced by permission of Taylor and Francis Group, LLC, a division of Informa plc..*

Figure 1.1: Bernhardt's (2018) multiple measures of data.

Bernhardt encourages teachers to use multiple measures where possible, and the more the better—two measures are better than one, and three measures are better than two. The greatest use of multiple measures is the overlap of all four types of data at the school level—for example, considering eighth-grade boys' perceptions of, and achievement in, a schoolwide targeted reading program. This analysis of the impact of the program would draw on demographics (a particular group of students), perceptions (the students' perceptions), student learning (results or improvements in reading), and school processes (the program itself). Bernhardt argues that combining multiple measures in this way provides a much better indicator of student and school success, as student learning results alone do not have any context associated with them.

PUBLICATION OF SCHOOL DATA

A key challenge of, and an argument against, using data to compare schools are the different socioeconomic factors and contextual features that affect a school's or student's performance.

In Australia, the My School website (www.myschool.edu.au) provides information for parents and the broader community on the performance of the school in recent standardized tests. This website reports on the Index of Community and Socio-Educational Advantage (ICSEA) score on each school's profile, but if the reader is unaware of what the ICSEA score means, it may not offer any additional assistance in his or her analysis or comparison. The website allows users to compare a particular school's result on the website to "all Australian schools" or "schools with similar students," but it is unwise to compare high-performing, selective private schools with small, underfunded local schools. In Australia, there is also a significant gap in educational outcomes between Indigenous and non-Indigenous students. Therefore, comparing the performance of a school in a remote Indigenous community with "schools with similar students" or "all Australian schools" would be pointless, and incredibly unfair on the teachers in the remote community that are working their hardest. Unfortunately, while well-intentioned in helping parents choose the best schooling option for their children, websites such as My School play into the fear and tracking mentality of some educators. Unfortunately, similar such websites exist in many countries around the world.

MEASURING PROGRESS AS WELL AS ACHIEVEMENT

Associated with the impact of socioeconomic status of students and the proportion of those who come from disadvantaged backgrounds is the emerging discussion of progress versus achievement measures. In contexts around the world, where the number of As achieved in subjects is celebrated or tertiary places are offered on a top-down model, the focus is often too much on achievement data and achievement measures. But measuring the amount of progress a student, teacher, or school makes, while requiring some information about starting points, is a better reflection of the impact that the school has had on the individual than only considering the score they achieve.

Discussing progress rather than achievement can be beneficial for a number of reasons. The first is that some schools administer difficult entrance examinations or are situated in a geographical area home to parents with high incomes and university degrees from prestigious universities. Both of these factors mean that achievement measures are not a fair comparison when it comes to comparing schools. While I do not want to go into the correlation between levels of education, income, and the likelihood of academic success for children at this point, the reality is that these factors can affect student performance. Hence, it is not fair to compare highly selective, wealthy schools with those that have students from low socioeconomic backgrounds with limited funds.

The second argument for focusing on progress rather than achievement is that high-performing students will often perform well, regardless of the quality of the teaching they are receiving. Therefore, if only achievement in schools is recognized, then it does little to reflect the effort or quality of the teaching that has occurred. I know I am in the dangerous space of potentially offending great teachers in high-performing schools, but this is not my intention. On the contrary, an argument against measuring progress over achievement for high-performing students is that A-grade students have little room to move in traditional grade boundaries compared with students achieving lower grades. For example, a C-grade student could improve by two whole grades to an A standard, but an A student can only move to an A+ or A-. While a student's knowledge and skills may improve remarkably because of the teaching, if he or she is already achieving an A, A+, or A-, there is little to no change that will be evident in his or her results.

Both achievement and progress measures have a place in our schools, and it is important that leaders are well versed in both. Students who are achieving the best results certainly deserve recognition and accolades, but it is important to ensure that we also recognize and celebrate the students who make significant improvements to their work ethic, approach, and results. They are just as worthy of attention and praise.

VALUE-ADDED MEASURES

In many school systems around the world, including the United States, England, and Italy, schools, systems, and governments refer to the progress made in schools through the use of the *value-added* measure. Value-added considers the amount that a school has added to individual students, classes, and cohorts, relative to the starting point of the students. This is an example of a progress measure rather than an achievement measure, and it is a way of recognizing and celebrating the teachers and schools that have the greatest impact.

In the United Kingdom, this progress measure is used regularly by teachers who work with *target grades* that have been set by a student's performance in standardized primary school assessments. While target grades can provide goal-setting motivation for students in some instances, there is much discussion about their applicability for subjects other than mathematics and English. In Italy, the value-added calculations are performed for students in grades 5, 8, and 10. School value-added scores are compared to regional and national comparisons and to "statistical neighbors" (Schleicher, 2019).

If your school is subject to value-added measures and comparisons, then you need to be fluent in the way that this measure is used and be able to support teachers who have questions or concerns about it. Value-added can actually be used well by teachers to track their own impact, to inform the best staffing choices for future years, and to compare impact to local or similar schools. Again, this is just one measure that is used in schools in different parts of the world—make sure you understand it if it affects you and your teachers.

SUMMARY

Because of international comparisons, the rise of data in use in other fields, and a desire for investors to achieve returns on their investments, schools around the world now have access to more data than ever before. While expectations regarding using student data are increasing for educators, there are varying degrees of use, skill, and training available. Consequently, teachers and school leaders are often in different places in their own data journey. All of these factors mean that using data well and leading data-informed change are complex tasks. Not only do administrators need to be skilled leaders; they must also lead in a data-informed context that includes progress and achievement measures, value-added measures, and international comparisons.

chapter two

THE CHALLENGE OF USING AND LEADING WITH DATA

BUT ISN'T DATA SCARY?

> *I've always been scared of data, but now I realise . . .*
> *data's not the enemy, data's my friend!*
> —*Workshop participant, PLC at Work® conference,*
> *Melbourne, 2019*

In my time as a teacher, leader, and consultant, I have met many teachers and school leaders who are philosophically opposed to the use and comparison of quantitative data in schools. Rightly or wrongly, some teachers and leaders feel as though they are personally being tracked, monitored, scrutinized, and held accountable for the achievement of their students. (In some instances, this is actually the case—the list of teachers with the highest value-added scores for their classes that was displayed in my school in the United Kingdom is proof that in some instances data are being used to survive rather than thrive.)

The resistance to the use of performance data at a school level, and the deprivatization of student performance data in international comparisons and national media, cascade down to the school and classroom level, where regular discussions about performance, achievement, and progress may not be commonplace. Further, a common argument that I have heard from people against the use of data in schools is that the numbers only tell us a small part of the story about the student, and so should not be used as they are such a minor piece of the puzzle. Other concerns stem from the way data are used to compare schools, and that it is a particularly difficult and unfair practice given the different sociocultural and socioeconomic features of schools. Australian educator Tim Hutton (2017) says that teachers have four key issues with data: (1) they have too much useless data, (2) the data are tainted, (3) teachers are not data analysts, and (4) data often do not lead to change.

In my work with teachers and leaders, I aim to allay some of their fears and to help educators see the benefits that an understanding of student data can have on their classroom and school, rather than focusing on the negatives. In fact, in my first book, *Using and Analysing Data in Australian Schools*, I talk about the importance of a growth mindset for teachers and leaders in using data, with respect to both their skills and the ability and potential of their students, and about the role that positive psychology has in this discussion on data.

Viewing student data through the lens of identifying the conditions in which our students and teachers flourish and thrive means that the analysis, visualization, and storytelling of the data take on an entirely new approach when compared with using data to fuel fears of tracking and accountability. But the reality is that teachers are tired and busy and do not necessarily have the skills needed to capitalize on the full potential of the data. In a 2019 study conducted by Mockler and Stacey, five hundred Australian teachers were surveyed about their views on data and evidence-based practices. Three statements from teachers about what the issues they have with data were highlighted:

> *Teachers are time poor. We are tired. It sounds good to do all this extra stuff, but unless we are given more time, it will just be another layer of pressure.*
>
> *Teachers believe in and want to rely on useful data, but they don't have the time to do it well.*
>
> *It must be practical, helpful, and not EXTRA.*

Even though you might be coming to data-informed change with the right mindset, the preceding quotes are a good reminder to leaders about the broad range of time pressures on teachers. Remember—perceptions are reality. If teachers believe they are too busy and cannot cope with what they see to be an additional layer of work or pressure, then you need to think about the ways that you can alleviate some of the pressure for them. Your efforts will support them, reduce some of the pressure, and show them that you recognize the increasing list of demands on them as educators.

NEGATIVITY BIAS

A factor that I believe is relevant to the discussion about the place of student data in schools and the negative perception of these data for some educators is a concept called *negativity bias* or *negativity dominance*. In *Thinking, Fast and Slow*, Daniel Kahneman (2011) discusses negativity dominance and the way in which one's motivation to achieve gains or improvements is not as strong as his or her motivation to avoid losses. Kahneman (2011) states:

> *Loss aversion refers to the relative strength of two motives: we are driven more strongly to avoid losses than to achieve gains. A reference point is sometimes the status quo, but it can also be a goal in the future: not achieving a goal is a loss, exceeding the goal is a gain. As we might expect from negativity dominance, the two motives are not equally powerful. The aversion to the failure of not reaching the goal is much stronger than the desire to exceed it. (pp. 302–303)*

> *Also, I learned to be aware that some people fear data for lots of reasons. Common ones were some people would often say data dehumanizes students; you're looking at numbers instead of students. There's a fear that'll be used almost as a weapon against their teaching, you know, accountability on steroids, so to speak. There is also a fear of new learnings and more things that they have to know and to do.*
> —Chris Mayes, principal

Therefore, if two outcomes (one good or neutral and one bad) are equally likely, negativity bias means that we will pay more attention to the negative outcome. In the data-informed landscape, negativity dominance could play a role in the perceptions that some staff have about data. We know that some staff see the use of data as a professionally enjoyable challenge, and they seek to improve their teaching and the learning of their students and track their impact. They—as the Bill and

Melinda Gates Foundation report (2015) classifies them—would be data mavens. But some teachers have negative perceptions about data in general, and they are concerned about how the data will look for their classes or how this will reflect on them. So, their motivation to avoid the negative (how the data might look or reflect on them) outweighs their desire to see the good and the potential in the data (how the data might positively affect them and their students). As Kahneman (2011) states, "The aversion to the failure . . . is much stronger than the desire to exceed it" (p. 303).

A concern about negativity dominance is the way in which teachers with this mind-set may approach or use the data for students in their care. In a recent interview with Chris Mayes, principal of St. Patrick's College, Shorncliffe, he said:

> The danger of data in the wrong hands is that it's misused, and it can be used to pigeonhole kids. And so, I think it's very important for us to make sure that our staff understand what they have and the purpose of why it's being used. There's no good getting a stanine reading, for instance, and saying, "Well, now I know the boy's stanine 5." That's okay, but "How do I get him into stanine 6?" is the bigger question, and "What does he need to do to get there?" You don't want teachers saying, "I knew he was always a B, and he will always remain a B." (C. Mayes, personal communication, June 11, 2019)

As Chris reminds us, when teachers think negatively about data, they can be misused. In this example, Chris refers to teachers who might see data as a limit of a student's ability or may assume that his or her past results are an indicator of how a student will inevitably perform for the rest of his or her schooling career. Neither of these assumptions is correct, and it is a leader's responsibility to work with teachers to understand not only the benefits of data but also the realistic limitations of point-in-time assessments that do not tell us about how a student will perform in the future.

There are so many factors that affect a student's performance at any given time. Motivations change, performance changes, and interests change over time. Humans evolve and grow at different rates in different areas and at different points in their lives. Data are useful, but always remember that they too will evolve and change as our students grow and change. On this topic, Carol Dweck (2008), in her book *Mindset: The New Psychology of Success*, reminds us that "test scores and measures of achievement tell you where a student is, but they don't tell you where a student could end up" (p. 34).

DATA LITERACY OF EDUCATORS

Regardless of the type or quality of the data that are collected in schools, they will never be put to proper use unless the data-informed educator is able to step through the process of collecting, visualizing, interpreting, understanding the needs of the learners in the classroom, and shifting his or her practice accordingly. In their webcast, Erin Junio, Darren Plumlee, Nandu Patil, and Tanvi Shah (2019) discuss the differences between, and the importance of, three key elements in the data journey: (1) data analysis, (2) data visualization, and (3) data storytelling. All three of these data literacy elements contribute to the skills of a data-informed teacher and leader, but they are terms that are not often used in the discussion on data in schools.

In this model, data analysis is what the presenters describe as the top of a big funnel. It involves the collection of data, using spreadsheeting programs, and crunching numbers. The second, data visualization—the middle part of the funnel—is when the data are turned into graphs, images, and other visual representations and are, in the presenters' words, made to look beautiful. Engagement with the data at this stage, they say, reduces the pain of the analysis in the previous stage, as the data look more visually pleasing and trends become more easily identifiable. The third stage, data storytelling, is the narrow, lowest part of the funnel, where users tap into their creativity, think about the audience and the issues they are facing, and look for what the data tell them about the problem. This is where the power lies in data—identifying how and why it can be useful to the organization in specific and actionable ways—but this is the point where there is the most risk of misinterpretation. It is important that the user and the storyteller of the data build their skills and ask questions about the data to ensure that the storytelling is as accurate as possible. As Tableau's analysts state, "Data tells you what's happening, but the story guides you to an understanding of why. And once you understand the cause, you can decide how to act" (Mackinlay, Kosara, & Wallace, 2013, p. 5). In addition, data storytelling allows us to make trends and insights less complex than they may appear otherwise (Fleming et al., 2019).

In a similar way, but by using different terminology, both Fisher and Good (2019) and Pringle (2019) emphasize that collecting data is only the first of three steps—analytics are the second step, and insights from the data are the third. Like the notion of storytelling, the use of the term *insights* for the third step is the point at which connections are identified between the trends in the data, real people, and challenges in the organization. By viewing the data in this way, insights emerge. Like Junio and colleagues' (2019) notion of storytelling, insights provide ideas for action that lead to transformation and add value to the organization. Regardless of whether or not you prefer to use the first set of terminology (analysis, visualization, storytelling) or the second (data, analytics, insights), the steps to being data informed are the same, and you need to understand these steps and build the skills of yourself and your teams in all three areas.

While it is important for leaders to be familiar with data analysis, visualization, and storytelling, the key to transforming organizations and schools is for leaders to be well versed in data storytelling. As educators with little background in statistics, analysis, and data visualizations, this may not seem to be something that comes naturally. But storytelling is something we all do and have always done. Outside of the data-informed schools context, Dougal Jackson and Jennifer Jackson (2018) state that leaders with strong storytelling skills often build better relationships with their staff and are more likely to have staff that buy in to the leader's vision because it has the power of giving ownership to the recipient. Further, using storytelling as a strategy means that it is more likely that staff will remember and act on the message. We all do this already! Although adding the data element into storytelling may not come easily, what is important is that we are proactive in our desire and processes to build these skills in ourselves and in our teams.

LEADING CHANGE

Implementing change is a constant, yet challenging, task for leaders in all fields, including in the field of education. But one of the key challenges in the change process can be knowing where to begin in the first place (Nussbaumer & Merkley, 2010).

In the school context, given that there are so many different factors that influence the organization and exist within the *black box* of classrooms and schools—and the fact that no two schools are the same—change and change leadership look different in each setting. This is challenging for leaders who are keen to drive school change and improvement but who are looking for a particular model or structure to follow. Often, school change and improvement are a process that develops from a collection of ideas picked up from the leader's previous experiences and adapted to the current setting, rather than a one-size-fits-all approach.

In their book, *How to Speak Human: A Practical Guide to Getting the Best From the Humans You Work With*, Jackson and Jackson (2018) focus on the importance of remembering our shared humanity through a change process. They state:

> *If change is hard for most folk, it's particularly tough on leaders. It's difficult to speak in certainties when we feel like we're only a step or two ahead of ourselves. It's challenging to chart a clear course of action for others when we're not entirely sure of what lies ahead. Through uncertain and foggy seas ahead, mates, human is our beacon. (Jackson & Jackson, 2018, p. xv)*

While the main goal of leading change in our schools is to encourage the modification of practices or processes that improve outputs and benefit students, it can also shift the culture of the organization depending on the size of the change effort.

Organizational culture is regularly described as *the way we do things around here* (see Burke & Litwin, 1992; Deal & Kennedy, 1982; Holbeche, 2006). So, as an extension of this, organizational change could be defined as transforming or altering *the way we do things around here*. True systemic change—that is, big change—alters the culture of a school or system by changing some of the underlying assumptions or institutional behaviors, processes, and products (Duffy & Reigeluth, 2008). Systemic change influences the entire institution, occurs intentionally over time, and ultimately results in the creation of a system that is continuously seeking an idealized vision of itself, as well as creating a future system that is substantially different from the current one (Bain & Swan, 2011).

In order to lead significant change at a school system level, the timing of the change effort needs careful consideration and planning. Duffy's (2008) work states, perhaps surprisingly, that the best time to implement large-scale transformational change in schools is when the system is performing well. This is somewhat contradictory to the common belief that change should occur when things are not going well in the school or system. Further, he identifies six characteristics required for transformational change to be successful on a large scale.

1. Leaders need to act on the basis of personal courage, passion, and vision, not on the basis of fear, self-survival, and self-interest.

2. Leaders and their followers must be willing and able to negotiate and push boundaries to create paradigm change—those who are rigid in their thinking and rule bound will not be successful.

3. Arguably most importantly, systemic change requires senior leaders to view their systems as a whole system, not as a collection of individual schools.

4. Change requires leaders and followers who are optimistic about the change and have a clear view of the opportunities that the proposed transformation offers the system.

5. Leaders and followers must possess the professional skills, motivation, and skills in leading change to be able to manage the process effectively.

6. Change requires human, technical, and financial resources that have been directed to the change process, to help sustain the change over a five- to seven-year period. This is the expected time period for large-scale change.

KOTTER'S CHANGE PROCESS

John Kotter is well known for the role he has played in the discussion on leading organizational change, as he has spent the last four decades working in this field. In this time, he has worked with organizations all around the world and has observed a range of organizations varying in size and turnover that attempted to make significant organizational change. As a result of his research and experience, he developed a series of eight steps for leading change.

Kotter found that—despite the best intentions—few change efforts had been successful, and he noted that it is important to realize that change goes through a series of phases that take a considerable amount of time. He also noted that error in one or more of those phases can have a devastating effect on the entire change process. Perhaps because we have relatively little experience in renewing organizations, Kotter (1995) states, "Very capable people often make at least one big error" (p. 60). Kotter (1995) used these errors to develop the series of eight steps for transforming an organization, and these steps have been reviewed and refined as Kotter's work has progressed. The current steps are depicted in figure 2.1. The steps are deliberately depicted in a circle as the process returns to the top—create a sense of urgency—after the previous change process has been followed and the change implemented.

The first step of Kotter's model, create a sense of urgency, identifies that leaders must first examine market and competitive realities in a change process, and thus identify and discuss crises, potential crises, and major opportunities early. In a data-informed school, this might include identifying the need for change, listing potential barriers, and assessing the opportunities.

The second step, build a guiding coalition, is concerned with assembling and encouraging a group of staff that can be influential and lead the change effort. In a school, this might be a data team or a curriculum or senior leadership team that are front and center of the change process.

Source: *Kotter, n.d. Reprinted with permission from Kotter, Inc.*
Figure 2.1: Kotter's eight-step change model.

The third step, form a strategic vision and initiatives, highlights the necessity for the guiding coalition to create a vision that directs the change effort and also develops strategies for achieving the vision. This process would be undertaken by the guiding coalition of teachers and middle or senior leaders in a school, who identify the vision and the plan for action.

The fourth step, enlist a volunteer army, uses every vehicle possible (namely, every method of communication available) to communicate the new vision and strategies to the rest of the organization. At this point, this is where the guiding coalition would bring the other teachers and school staff into the change process, teach new behaviors, and share with them the vision and approaches through information sessions, professional development sessions, meetings, and newsletters.

The fifth step, enable action by removing barriers, removes obstacles such as systems and structures that undermine or contradict the vision for the change, and encourages others to take risks and embrace nontraditional ideas, activities, and actions.

The sixth step, generate short-term wins, highlights the necessity to monitor progress and improvements so that employees can be recognized and rewarded when the improvements occur. In schools, when teachers, middle leaders, or senior leaders in the change team see improvement, they should share the success in all-staff forums and meetings.

The seventh step, sustain acceleration, uses increased credibility and the momentum of the change to change other systems, structures, and policies that do not fit the vision. This stage involves hiring, promoting, and developing employees who can implement the vision, and reinvigorating the process with new processes, themes, and change agents.

Finally, the eighth step, institute change, involves articulating the connections between the new behaviors as a result of the change and the positive outcomes and successes. In the school context, this would involve the principal communicating evidence of successes to all staff and highlighting the contribution of the people in the team. This step leads back to the first step, creating a sense of urgency, to begin the next change cycle.

While Kotter's focus was on systemic transformational change for a broader organizational context, as a result of the way in which he researched and constructed these eight steps, this process could almost be used as a direct checklist for leaders to follow to drive change in their school. It is important to acknowledge that although these steps may appear to simplify the process of transformational change, all organizational reform (including change in schools) is a challenging task and must be done with consideration of context, people, and policies around which the organization is situated.

DATA WISE PROJECT

In terms of leading change in a data-informed school context, a resource available to teachers and leaders is the Data Wise Project, run by the Harvard University Graduate School of Education since 2006. In their description of the program, the university states:

> *The mission of the Data Wise Project is to support educators in using collaborative data inquiry to drive continuous improvement of teaching and learning for all students. Our vision is that every educator around the world is part of a thriving learning community that ensures that all students develop the skills, knowledge, and dispositions that will allow them to live joyful and rewarding lives. (Harvard Graduate School of Education, n.d.)*

The focus of the Data Wise Project is on teaching teams and teachers working together to analyze and respond to data.

As visible in the Data Wise improvement process in figure 2.2, the process involves educators following a series of eight steps from beginning the work to acting and assessing the progress made through the three main phases (prepare, inquire, act).

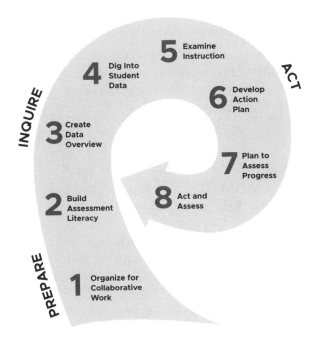

Source: *Boudett, City, & Murnane, 2013, p. 5. Reprinted with permission from Harvard Education Press, an imprint of Harvard Education Publishing Group.*

Figure 2.2: The Data Wise improvement process.

1. Organize for collaborative work. At this stage, educators develop structures and teams in the school that enable the data analysis process to occur. They create expectations for the team, including team norms, and organize a plan for the timing of the collaborative work.

2. Build assessment literacy. Teachers and leaders build their understanding and their comfort with the data. At this stage, participants learn about the types of data collected and about the dangers of the misuse of data.

3. Create data overview. Participants develop an inquiry or priority question and display the data in ways that support analysis. They investigate data, identify trends, and begin to make sense of the data.

4. Dig into student data. From this understanding of the student data, educators formulate a student-centered problem. They modify the initial inquiry question they devised in the previous step to make it student centered and more specific to the issue that they identified in the data.

5. Examine instruction. Participants identify a problem with the teaching practice. This issue is associated with the priority question generated in step 3 and the student-centered problem in step 4. Teachers develop a shared understanding of the practices and the impact of the teaching on the data and begin to think about the ways in which they could shift pedagogy in order to bring about change.

6. Develop action plan. Practitioners create a future plan that indicates the anticipated changes in pedagogy. They put this plan in writing, include the instructional practices that they will utilize, and state how this will look in classrooms.

7. Plan to assess progress. This stage involves short-, medium-, and long-term planning. It requires the team to determine the way in which they will assess progress along the change journey as well as the goals that they have set for student learning.

8. Teachers act and assess the pedagogical impact of the change. What improvements have educators made to teaching and learning, and what should they modify further? They celebrate successes at this point and modify and adjust the plan as required. (Bocala, 2013; Oberman & Boudett, 2015)

The Data Wise Project has reportedly been used in many schools and districts in the United States (Oberman & Boudett, 2015). A strength of this program is that it was developed in conjunction with teachers and leaders from the Boston Public Schools, so it has roots in real pedagogical practice and actual classrooms. It is also focused on outcomes and walks educators progressively through the plan, which is a definite strength of the program. While leaders can use the process, many of the success stories are from teachers and teaching teams, rather than schoolwide cultural change. But the process does offer tangible steps for teachers and leaders to follow.

PROFESSIONAL LEARNING COMMUNITIES (PLCS)

Another area relating to leading change in schools specifically (but not solely a data program) is the notion of professional learning communities (PLCs). While PLCs have been studied since the 1960s—most notably since the publication of *Professional Learning Communities at Work: Best Practices for Enhancing Student Achievement* by Richard DuFour and Robert Eaker in 1998—PLCs gained momentum in the 2010s after proving to be an effective way to lead change in schools. The PLC method is a school- and systemwide approach to raising the quality of teaching and learning in schools, and data play a key role in the improvement process. The concept of PLCs takes a few different forms, depending on the resource that one is reading, but the three big ideas that drive the work of the PLC process in a key contribution in this area—*Learning by Doing: A Handbook for Professional Learning Communities at Work, Third Edition*

(DuFour, DuFour, Eaker, Many, & Mattos, 2017)—are (1) a focus on learning; (2) a collaborative culture and collective responsibility; and (3) a results orientation.

The goal of a PLC is to ensure high levels learning and achievement for all students, but in *Learning by Doing,* the authors make it clear that a PLC is not merely a program or a project with a small group of staff, or simply the arrangement of small teams of people meeting together—it is a way of life. In fact, "it is ongoing—a continuous, never-ending process of conducting schooling that has a profound impact on the structure and culture of the school and the assumptions and practices of the professionals within it" (DuFour et al., 2017, p. 10).

In terms of this discussion on the use and analysis of data in schools, using data is particularly important to the first and third big ideas of a PLC (a focus on learning and a results orientation). While data-informed leadership sits well within the entire PLC process, these two big ideas in particular require data-informed skills and leadership. Under the umbrella of these three big ideas sit nine core elements (DuFour et al., 2017).

1. Defining a clear and compelling purpose
2. Building the collaborative culture of a professional learning community
3. Creating a results orientation in a professional learning community
4. Establishing a focus on learning
5. Creating team-developed common formative assessments
6. Responding when some students don't learn
7. Hiring, orienting, and retaining new staff
8. Addressing conflict and celebrating in a professional learning community
9. Implementing the professional learning community process systemwide

Again, data are vitally important to these nine core elements of a PLC—particularly in elements 3, 5, and 6. Further, PLCs utilize four critical questions to drive their collective inquiry and action research.

1. What do we want students to learn?
2. How will we know if they have learned?
3. What will we do if they don't learn?
4. What will we do if they already know it?

The key way to answer these questions is through the use, analysis, visualization, and storytelling of data.

Kotter's eight-step process, the Data Wise Project, and the PLC process provide guidance for educators on ways in which data-informed change and improvement could occur in schools. Ultimately, all three structures seek to enable organizations to improve, albeit in different ways.

PRIMING THE ENVIRONMENT FOR DATA-INFORMED CHANGE

> *The teams we'll lead in the very near future (if we haven't already) will be vastly different. As leaders, the ability to go beyond our technical expertise and embrace our human skills will be what keeps us relevant: inspiring people to do their best work; helping them navigate change; promoting problem solving and innovation; keeping them safe, healthy and happy. Making a difference. Creating a legacy. These are the hallmarks of a leader skilled in the art of influence. —Jackson & Jackson, 2018, p. xxvi*

The purpose of this resource is to provide guidance to educational leaders about the ways in which they can lead data-informed change in their learning communities. Prior to the discussion of the steps that should be followed through this process, it is important to recognize some cultural and environmental elements that are vital for the change process to be successful. I call these elements of the culture *priming the environment* because they are cultural and environmental traits that the leader can reflect on and consciously build, prior to the change taking place and throughout the process of change itself. By considering these elements, the school and work culture will be more conducive to change, and the change effort will be more effective.

The harsh reality is that there are some schools in which change will be incredibly difficult to enact because the culture, history, or capacity of teachers and leaders is not conducive to the process. By actively trying to *prime the environment*, you are setting your school up for more success than you may have had otherwise. It is possible that some change might take place in a toxic, negative work environment, but if it does, it would be characterized by fear and accountability, and without true buy-in from staff. Change in this instance might occur in small pockets, because teachers and leaders are fearful of not taking part, but it would certainly not be widespread or sustainable over the longer term. On the other hand, building and sustaining a positive change culture in your school mean that you are more likely to have people genuinely buy in and take part in the change, and even lead the process for you.

You may already do many of the things discussed in these elements of priming the environment—your environment might even already be primed in many ways—so this is a chance to reflect on the way these attributes affect effective data-informed leadership. Learning from previous reform efforts can and should always influence future reform efforts, and it is my hope that this discussion contributes to this conversation in the increasingly data-informed school systems in which we work.

The experiences that I have had in leading teams through data-informed change as a learning area leader, as a leader of curriculum across the school, and as a consultant have shaped my understanding of what works when attempting to lead change in schools. As a leader and as a practitioner, I have always tried to learn from others, and have tried to emulate and reproduce the things that I have seen work. Over time, I have learned that twelve key elements are required for a leader to prime the environment or build a culture that will enable him or her to lead data-informed change. These elements are:

1. Talking about the data
2. Starting with the why
3. Being transparent
4. Embracing the power of vulnerability
5. Building professional trust
6. Encouraging curiosity
7. Reaching a critical mass or the tipping point
8. Leaning into difficult conversations
9. Leading up and down
10. Establishing a data team
11. Building a culture of predicting results
12. Celebrating small wins

While many of these elements can be found in organizational change resources, psychology, or leading change literature, they haven't been grouped in this manner or discussed in the context of requirements in priming a data-informed context in an educational setting. The data-informed educational context is, after all, relatively new for some school systems and can be quite different from other employment sectors.

Although these twelve elements are listed from most to least influential, all of them are incredibly important. The omission of one or more of the elements would reduce the impact of the leader and potentially the entire change process. For example, if there is lack of professional trust, transparency will be reduced, it will be harder to reach the critical mass of people required to lead the change, and it will be incredibly difficult to lead both up and down. Similarly, if you are unwilling or unable to embrace difficult conversations, you will lose respect and trust from members of your team, it will be difficult to build a guiding coalition of people to help you achieve your goals, and there will be fewer wins to celebrate. The twelve factors required for priming the environment, and the relationships between them, can be seen in figure 2.3. Without just one piece, the circle would be incomplete.

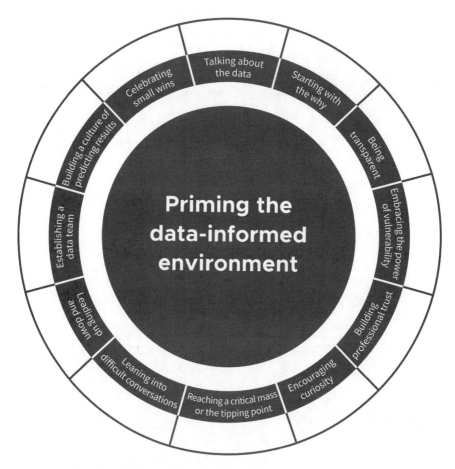

Figure 2.3: Twelve key elements for priming the environment.

You will also notice that many of these requirements for priming the data-informed environment (with the exception of element 1) are cultural characteristics that are difficult to quantify or measure—that is, a leader couldn't simply peruse the list and tick a box to say he or she has completed it. Some might argue that some of the elements are able to be measured, in that the leader might say, "OK, element 1 is done—I spoke about the data," or "I celebrated some small wins last week," but none of these elements are an "event" that happens once and then is forgotten about. They need to continue consistently before, during, and after the change process—they need to become a part of *what we do around here*. Because of the fluid nature of schools and the necessity for these priming elements to occur regularly, there is no value in adding a timeline or an expectation of when or how frequently these things will occur—they need to occur in a way that is authentic, responsive, and timely.

THE TEN-STEP CHANGE PROCESS

While effective leadership and a conducive school climate are important for leading data-informed change, a key learning from my initial experience as a school data consultant is that moving through the stages of data-informed change is, indeed, the hardest part. Although some teachers and leaders might still be learning the best ways to collect and analyze data, more often people understand the data and can analyze and develop visualizations of them but get bogged down in the analysis and storytelling and do not know how to (or that they should) get out of their spreadsheets and into the real world to create tangible change. Some leaders, perhaps implicitly or explicitly, believe that a knowledge of or exploration of the data will lead to change in itself. Unfortunately, this is not the case.

While the first part of data-informed change is building data literacy and analysis skills, it is only the initial step in the process. There are a host of learning management systems that generate graphs and longitudinal performance imagery and do a lot of the organization and visual representations of data for us. But no matter how wonderful an individual's data literacy and analysis skills, the program's capabilities, the graphs, or the hours invested in spreadsheets or tables of values, none of this leads to data-informed change unless the user moves along a data-informed change continuum and actively translates the data into storytelling and steps for improvement.

Moving from having data to leading change requires a series of ten steps. Each of these steps is dependent on the previous one—the cycle leads back to the first step—and is vital to the process. If one of the stages was to be omitted, the data-informed change would be far less likely to succeed and would potentially not be able to progress further through the process. The relationship between the steps can be represented in a circle of ten steps, with each step being a part of the jigsaw—without one, the circle would be incomplete.

As illustrated in figure 2.4 (page 42), the leader and his or her team members must understand the types of data available and what they mean prior to undertaking any data-informed change. This includes summary statistics but also an understanding of the way the data were collected and the reasons and goals behind the collection.

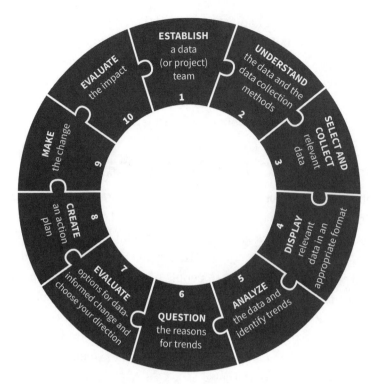

Figure 2.4: The ten-step data-informed change process.

Following this, the team needs to select and collect the data that are relevant for the analysis being undertaken, and then display these data in an appropriate format so they can be analyzed. Once they have analyzed the data and recognized the trends, the team must brainstorm ideas about the reasons for the identified trends and then explore available options for data-informed change. With a list of possible reasons and options, the team is then able to make informed decisions about the changes that need to and will be made, carving out an action plan for the change process itself. They then make the change and, throughout the change process, evaluate the impact at regular intervals to track the progress of the change.

The goals of this ten-step process are to provide a mechanism by which schools can direct their change process and support their analysis along the way. The work of Kotter, the Data Wise Project, and the approach of PLCs, as well as school experience and the work of Patrick Lencioni (2002), inform one way in which schools can tackle the challenge of data-informed change. Ideally, these ten steps sit within a primed environment, so the process is supported by effective cultural and environmental conditions.

SUMMARY

Many educators find it difficult to understand how they should progress through the stages of identifying trends in data to leading tangible change. By actively and consciously priming the environment for change and progressing through the ten-step change process, leaders are more likely to succeed in their change efforts. The following ten chapters discuss each of the steps, including links to the relevant literature and real school examples. When relevant, the twelve factors for priming the environment (see figure 2.3, page 40) are discussed to explain the importance of these conditions on the change effort.

chapter three

ESTABLISH A DATA
(OR PROJECT) TEAM

> *Factfulness is . . . recognising that a single perspective can limit your imagination, and remembering that it is better to look at problems from many angles to get a more accurate understanding and find practical solutions.*
> —Dr. Hans Rosling

If you are trying to lead significant school change by using and analyzing data, the first step that you need to embark on is establishing a *data team* or *project team*. For some schools, a team that focuses on a particular change project may be the best option, and in others, a school-based data team will embark on a range of projects. It is up to you which one you choose to establish, but this is the first decision that you need to make with your leadership team on this journey.

PRIMING THE ENVIRONMENT BY ESTABLISHING A DATA TEAM

Data teams have the potential to orient the broader teaching team toward the goal, as the data team helps steer the ship in the right direction through this time of significant change. As Dr. Hans Rosling and colleagues (2018) state in *Factfulness*, looking at problems from a range of perspectives leads to a more accurate understanding and to useful and practical solutions. Participation of a range of staff in your data team capitalizes on a range of perspectives and ensures a more robust and accurate understanding of the issues.

> *Having a data team makes sure that the data is accessible to everyone that needs it, not cards to the chest of the leadership team. . . . It defeats the purpose of talking about data, and limits the impact on teaching, if the teachers don't get to use it and understand it.*
> —*Chris Mayes, principal*

Data teams work in the school context for a number of reasons. When well-organized and well-led, the team collectively reviews and analyzes the data, brainstorms solutions to identified issues, prioritizes steps for action, co-constructs the storytelling, and encourages team members to consult their sphere of influence to learn more and lead change themselves. At the data team level, it builds the analytical skills of the group and encourages members to see the data from different perspectives. It is sometimes important to be able to see the way in which others interpret data or justify or explain a result, because it teaches us more about the data and how we could or should approach the storytelling.

Data analysis and interpretation conversations in the data team positively influence the team members as they promote thinking slowly and rationally about a reason or response, or *system 2 thinking* (see Kahneman, 2011). This is in contrast to utilizing system 1 thinking and jumping to a potentially quick and inaccurate conclusion (Kahneman, 2011). But, ultimately, a data team is beneficial because one person never has all the answers. Data teams work because different people can interpret the same thing in different ways. When educators seek multiple perspectives, conversations follow, and the team can devise the best solutions. In the same way, rarely does one factor ever contribute to a particular result or trend. Therefore, having a team of people sit around and mull over the data, the reasons, and the options means that the action plan can be based on more rigorous analysis, and more well-thought-out solutions.

Finally, when a team is considering the data, analyzing trends, and identifying next steps and an action plan, the more people you have in that team, the better. If your data team is made up of curriculum middle leaders, pastoral middle leaders, senior leaders, and teachers, they will go on to enact change for you in their realm of influence. They will help you get to the critical mass that you will rely on later in the change process because they will have a better understanding of the data and will talk about them and the changes in the lunchroom, at staff meetings, and in their departments. They will recruit followers for you.

TEAM COMMITMENTS

While establishing your data team, it is vital that you follow four key commitments with and for your team. The people in your data team are giving up their own time (or planning time) to be involved in the initiative, so you have a couple of key responsibilities to them to show that you value their contribution. You should:

1. Co-construct team assumptions and norms
2. Keep your meetings to an appropriate length
3. Ensure meetings always have a well-planned agenda
4. Ensure meetings are effectively chaired

These four commitments will go a long way to keeping your team members active and engaged.

> *First of all, I think that what I did learn is that before you start to make any significant change, you need to make sure that everyone's on the same page, and therefore understands that everyone will have different assumptions about data. And so what we need to do is to be very clear with what our vision is, as to what data we want to use and how we want to use it. And therefore, from that there's got to be the creation of a very clear and aspirational vision that is constantly reminding people why they're here.*
> —Chris Mayes, principal

ASSUMPTIONS ABOUT DATA

Co-constructing team assumptions and team norms is an important way to start your data team and set the tone for the way in which data conversations will occur. In the introduction to this book, I presented the views and perceptions on data that I bring to this conversation.

- Data provide us with information about student potential (which can sometimes be different from what we thought).
- Everyone can learn and improve with effort and application.

- Using data can motivate and engage students.
- Data can be inaccurate and may not truly reflect a student's ability.
- Data should be used to inform planning, programs, and differentiation.
- Data can surprise us, for the right reasons.
- Data should be used not to catch teachers out but to catch students out—whether they are underperforming, flying under the radar, or achieving great results.

As a result of these beliefs and assumptions, I would come to a data team meeting with a mindset different from that of someone who did not hold similar views or did not have as much experience with data as I have had. The views that I hold are not necessarily right, and someone else's are not wrong—they are different, and it is important to recognize and celebrate the differences that we have in our teams. It is also important to acknowledge the place that others come from in their data journey, because by understanding others, we can work with them, we can be challenged by different ideas, and we can challenge them where necessary.

In *Using and Analysing Data in Australian Schools*, I talked about co-constructing a list of assumptions with your team by having individuals answer the following questions.

- Why will data be useful for you?
- What do you think data can add in your context?
- What can data teach you that may not have been previously visible?
- What are your core beliefs about learner potential?

These questions are useful in orienting your team to the data-informed context. What do your team members actually believe? What baggage do they bring with them? Answering these questions and having an open conversation about their perceptions become a learning opportunity for the group and an opportunity to see how individuals believe data should and could be used in the school—and then, about how those data conversations should occur in the new team space.

Once individuals have answered these questions and you have discussed the answers as a team, co-construct a list of collaborative team assumptions on data. Outline how you will approach the data-informed conversations as a team. Once you have agreed on the conventions for your team, have all data team members commit to these statements, and even have them sign the statement of assumptions if possible. The benefit of having a shared commitment or understanding about the belief that the team has about data is that if the team deviates from this shared understanding at any time, it is easy to redirect their attention to the document that they had all previously agreed on (and it provides a structure for you to return to when you are having any difficult conversations!).

DEVELOPMENT OF TEAM NORMS

Alongside the discussion of the team assumptions about data sits the importance of developing team norms. Team norms create the opportunity for staff to build a framework around the commitments that they make to themselves and other members of the team regarding the way they will work and operate. Team norms provide a structure by which leaders can direct conversations, interactions, and approaches to issues and challenges. There has been much written about the development of team norms or protocols, including in the Data Wise Project and the professional learning community space.

The first step of the Data Wise process—organize for collaborative work—guides educators through a process of creating team norms during the preparation phase. The goal of norms in the Data Wise process is for the team to build a set of commitments that they all agree to, which outlines how they intend to work with one another. Best practice with team norms is that the team regularly refers to and revises the norms, uses them, and follows through when the norms are not followed.

Lyn Sharratt (2018) discusses the importance of having a set of operating norms in a community of practice in order to clearly articulate expectations. She also believes that it is important for team members to co-construct the norms or protocols so they have ownership over the commitments they are making. Some sample protocols offered by Sharratt (2018) are as follows.

- Everyone's voice is important—we listen respectfully.
- Being respectful in our engagement builds strong working relationships that lead to empowerment.
- We reflect on our work as we learn with and from each other.
- In collaborating, we empower our own learning and the learning of our colleagues.
- We build learning capacity together.
- Collaborating authentically builds confidence and success.
- We persevere—we believe all students can learn and all teachers can teach with impact given the right time and support.
- We believe in our interdependence to achieve students' learning goals.
- Having shared beliefs and understandings about student achievement guides our work. (p. 13)

In their work on PLCs, DuFour and colleagues (2017) state that team norms help to build trust, commitment, and accountability. They provide six tips for creating team norms, suggesting the following.

1. Each team should create its own norms.

2. Norms should be stated as commitments to act or behave in certain ways rather than as beliefs.

3. Norms should be reviewed at the beginning and end of each meeting for at least six months.

4. Teams should formally evaluate their effectiveness at least twice a year.

5. Teams should focus on a few essential norms rather than creating an extensive laundry list.

6. One of the team's norms should clarify how the team will respond if one or more members are not observing the norms.

The PLC's norms guidance calls for protocols that are clear, focused on behaviors and actions, and used regularly. For instance, the authors note that "the statement, 'We will arrive to meetings on time and stay fully engaged throughout the meeting,' is more powerful than, 'We believe in punctuality'" (DuFour et al., 2017, p. 75). This is valuable advice.

Using norms at the beginning and end of each meeting for the first six months ensures that the use of norms becomes part of the culture, and including a norm that addresses the response if a norm is not observed ensures that there is clarity around who will deal with an issue when it arises, and how they will deal with it.

LENGTH, AGENDA, AND CHAIRING OF MEETINGS

Your second, third, and fourth commitments to your team are that you ensure meetings are kept to an appropriate length, that they have an agenda, and that they are chaired appropriately. I think we've all sat through enough meetings that have not moved quickly, have descended into individual conversations or complaints, or have had us leave the meeting at the end wondering why we ever carved the time out of our day to be involved. It is from this experience that we know why these commitments are important.

People such as Donna McGeorge (2018) have written books like *The 25 Minute Meeting* on the necessity for short, effective, and strategic meetings in organizations and the ways to make these happen. For this reason, it is vital that you have a plan for your data team meetings, ensure that they have a clear agenda, and elect a chairperson who keeps the group in check. Ultimately, in each meeting you want your team members reporting back, moving through new business, and moving on quickly and efficiently. Estimate the amount of time you will need to do this, and allocate that amount of time to begin with. If, after a while, you can shorten the time, then do so. But ensure that your meeting lengths, agendas, and chairperson keep your meetings effective and punchy. If you don't, your team members will not hang around for long.

CHOOSING TEAM MEMBERS

The most important consideration in establishing a data team is the people that you recruit for it, because they will determine its success. In the data teams that I have been involved in, there has been a deliberate mix of senior leaders, curriculum middle leaders, pastoral middle leaders, and teachers, and I strongly encourage you to seek a similar mix. If there is a member of your teaching team who you believe would be a beneficial contributor to the team but he or she doesn't express interest initially, don't be afraid to tap the person on the shoulder and encourage his or her participation. You never know where that conversation may lead!

In most of the schools that I have worked in, participation in the data team was voluntary, but it was encouraged for middle and senior leaders. Teachers were welcome to join the team if data were a particular area of interest for them. Participation in the team was a yearly commitment, with meetings before or after school, and anyone was welcome to be involved if he or she was happy to commit to the full year.

It is also important to determine the frequency and timing of the meetings that you will hold for your data team. In one school that I worked in, we used to meet twice a term before school at 7:30 a.m. on a day where no other meetings were scheduled. When looking for interest from your team, you will need to have a plan for when you are scheduling time for the meetings, as this will determine whether certain people have this time available and therefore are able to be involved.

With respect to the time commitment required of your team members, you will also need to consider whether you need time set aside for a strategic visioning/planning meeting at any stage during the year. At one school I worked in, we did this every six months, usually during student-free days at the beginning of the semester in a two-hour block. Again, this requires some planning and awareness around the amount of time that you will need, *why* you need the time, and what you hope to get out of it. It is also important that your team members know all of this before they make the commitment. Be up front and transparent from the beginning about what their commitment means in terms of time.

Another consideration for your data team is whether or not you should use an external consultant in the initial stages to help you get started over the first six to twelve months. If you are unsure how to lead your team in this space or are not convinced that you have anyone in your team that could run the process, consider an external data, change, or leadership consultant to support your work. Often, an external set of eyes can offer a useful perspective or suggestions that you might not have otherwise considered. Similarly, it is sometimes easier for an external consultant to ask the difficult questions and have difficult conversations that might benefit your school in the short term.

COLLECTIVE TEACHER EFFICACY

The development of a data team capitalizes on the role of collective teacher efficacy in your school, rather than many individuals working toward different goals.

Since the publication of his seminal work *Visible Learning* in 2008, John Hattie has conducted meta-analyses of educational studies to determine the effect size of a range of factors that influence student learning, both inside and outside of the "black box." In an update to his list of factors that influence student learning, Hattie listed 256 factors and their effect size in an effort to rank and position the top 256 factors affecting student outcomes (Visible Learning Plus, 2017). In general, Hattie refers to 0.4 effect size as being the *hinge point* at which a particular strategy has a greater effect than the progress expected from a student in a regular year of growth. Therefore, the higher the effect size (and the further above 0.4), the greater impact the strategy could have on a student. Anything below 0.4 is not particularly worth investing effort in, as it would not lead to the amount of growth expected in a regular school year.

The most interesting thing to come out of Hattie's update is that *collective teacher efficacy* now sits at the top of his list as the most effective factor, with an effect size of 1.57. Hattie explains that collective teacher efficacy is a combination of teachers working together to improve student achievement and also believing it is possible to improve. In discussing collective teacher efficacy, Douglas Fisher, Nancy Frey, and John Almarode (as cited in Corwin, 2019) state:

> *When teachers come together and they have procedures in place, structures in place, protocols in place, and they have high expectations for themselves and their learners, and they build that sense of collective "we are in this and can do this," nothing stops them.*

The effect size of collective teacher efficacy is more than double that of the impact of feedback (0.7 effect size) and triple that of effective teacher-student relationships (0.52 effect size).

While some educators question the accuracy and relevance of Hattie's rank order (largely because of the different numbers of studies used, and the fact that it relies on averages), I believe it is a useful tool. Although the reliance on averages does have some limitations (as it does not show the spread of the impact, and some interventions within each of the 256 factors may be much higher or much lower than the average effect size indicates), I do not believe there is a better way of calculating what works better in schools than this effect size model. In a climate where we cannot do everything and we need to maximize the effect from the effort we are putting in, Hattie's ranking gives some order to the things that work better in schools than in others, and it directs teachers' attention to strategies that are actually useful, rather than investing time in the wrong things.

AN EXAMPLE OF THE IMPACT OF COLLECTIVE TEACHER EFFICACY

Although as a leader of data-informed teams and change, I had not explicitly considered collective teacher efficacy until I heard of it reaching the top of Hattie's effect size list, I realized that I have witnessed the impact of collective teacher efficacy numerous times as a teacher and as a leader. In a school I taught in on Brisbane's north side in Queensland, Australia, I helped stream, or group by ability, the students in the middle years, as there were significant differences in ability levels across the year groups. This was to help teachers with their differentiation, so that the spread was smaller in each class group. I was one of four learning area teachers—comprising mathematics, science, English, and religious education—for a particular group of grade 9 students. Collectively, we aimed to raise academic expectations, implement consistent practices across classrooms, and insist on similar expectations with respect to work ethic and behavior.

Some of the students in the class had historically been difficult to manage at times; they were loud and energetic and did not overly value any investment of time and effort into their studies. But within the first term after the change in core teachers and the increased (and consistent) expectations, the four of us could see noticeable changes in the students' work ethic and behavior. While some lessons were better than others (and some made me question the progress I thought we were making), it was clear that while we might have been taking the occasional step back, we were definitely moving forward.

I witnessed a real moment of achievement in the last two weeks of the school year, when we allocated eight lessons to revision and preparation for the final exam, which assessed all the ninth-grade mathematics content. During one lesson in the revision period, I sat back and looked around. All students were studying independently with their headphones on, completely focused on what they were doing, or were in a pair or group, supporting one another to revise and learn the content. They were showing each other how to approach a problem and how to try to solve it, even when they didn't necessarily know if they could get to the answer. There were students solving problems (and arguing about different ways to solve them) on the whiteboard at the front of the room. In those last two weeks, lessons like that one proved the value of the efforts that the four of us had invested in this group over the year.

The class effort was noticeable outside the classroom too. Other teachers commented that they saw students studying for the mathematics exam outside school time (something they had never seen before!). One member of the staff said that in all their time at the school, they had never seen any student particularly interested in succeeding in mathematics, but now they saw many students from across the year level working hard to be successful. By the end of the semester, significant changes were evident. However, this story isn't some magical turnaround. There were still times when the grade 9 group was off-task and challenging, but the vast majority of lessons were effective and focused on progress and growth, and behavior was rarely an issue.

While I have always had aspirations of motivating this type of change in my classroom, I could not have made the changes that I saw in that year if I had tried to do it alone. Rather than being one of this group's six learning area teachers who had particular expectations of them, four of their six teachers had exactly the same expectations. The fact that the students were hearing a consistent message from four of their teachers, day in, day out, had an impact on their learning, effort, and progress, and a much greater impact than one person would have had alone. It was not a miracle—it was the little things that we did, and the frequency in which the students were exposed to the higher expectations, that had an impact. This, for me, is a perfect example of the collective teacher efficacy that Hattie talks about.

So, as the person who initiates the data or project team in your school, you need to be aware of the role that collective teacher efficacy has on progress and achievement and harness its power in your team. For example, promoting the importance of a year-level teaching team working and planning together, or having a group of teachers across learning areas focus their efforts on a particular group of students, harnesses the power of collective teacher efficacy. Similarly, by creating a team around you to work toward the change, you are harnessing the power of collective teacher efficacy to create an impact on student achievement far greater than if you attempted it alone.

Increasingly, research is indicating that this is the most powerful school-based factor—why not capitalize on it?

COLLABORATION VERSUS COOPERATION

At this point it is important to point out a clear difference between collaboration and cooperation, and the importance of promoting a culture of collaboration right from the initial stages of your data team, rather than cooperation. Ann Marie Thomson, James L. Perry, and Theodore K. Miller (2007) used the work of Donna J. Wood and Barbara Gray (1991) to define collaboration:

> *Collaboration is a process in which autonomous or semi-autonomous actors interact through formal and informal negotiation, jointly creating rules and structures governing their relationships and ways to act or decide on the issues that brought them together; it is a process involving shared norms and mutually beneficial interactions. (p. 25)*

Data teams should be focused on collaboration—where team members learn together and work together, and the skills of each individual contribute to the overall success of the team. Cooperation in schools looks a lot like compliance, following instructions, and toeing the party line. That is not what you want in your data team—you want healthy and constructive conflict and conversation, where people respectfully challenge the ideas of the others, see themselves as a part of the team, and know that they all have an equal part to play in its success. This is not and should never be about a leader running the team with no input from the team members.

To build collaboration rather than cooperation, you need to hand over some (if not all) of the roles and responsibilities of your project to others in your data team, value the contribution of all members, and show your team that you trust them and are learning alongside them. In their work on collaboration, Wood and Gray (1991) and Thomson and colleagues (2007) highlight the importance of autonomy and interaction. Help the members of your team determine their role in the process and encourage interaction between participants and build autonomy.

GRIT, GROWTH MINDSET, AND POSITIVE PSYCHOLOGY

> *The message is that there are no "knowns." There are things we know that we know. There are known unknowns. That is to say there are things that we now know we don't know. But there are also unknown unknowns. There are things we don't know we don't know. So, when we do the best we can and we pull all this information together, and we then say, well, that's basically what we see as the situation, that is really only the known knowns and the known unknowns. And each year, we discover a few more of those unknown unknowns. It sounds like a riddle. It isn't a riddle. It is a very serious, important matter.*
> —Donald Rumsfeld, former U.S. Secretary of Defense, speaking on the "Global War on Terrorism"

In *Using and Analysing Data in Australian Schools*, I discussed the importance of three factors that I believe are key to using data well—(1) grit, (2) growth mindset, and (3) positive psychology. Grit is the willingness to persist and get things done, particularly through challenging or adverse scenarios, and it is key to learning any new skill or approach or achieving new goals. A growth mindset is the belief that intelligence is not fixed and that, with work and learning, intelligence develops. Positive psychology is the area of study that investigates the conditions that lead to human flourishing. It is important in a data-informed world because it is vital that leaders recognize and celebrate the great things that they find in the data as well as identify the areas that require attention. As an individual and as a leader in schools, I wholeheartedly believe in the importance of these three elements affecting the way in which you operate as an individual practitioner and the way in which you lead.

While as an individual you should be learning, persisting, and looking for the conditions that work best for others, as a leader it is even more important that you model and encourage others to adopt similar mindsets and approaches. If you lead by example and demonstrate grit, a growth mindset, and a focus on positive conditions and outcomes within your data team, the members of your team are more likely to follow you and be inspired to adopt a similar approach. If you expect other people to persist and learn new skills but are unwilling to do so yourself, and you continually focus on negative outcomes and expect others to take the lead on projects, then your team will more than likely follow you in that way also.

For this reason, it is vital that you know your strengths and weaknesses as a leader, that you know how to articulate your vision—particularly to your initial change team—and that you are aware that you must model the behaviors and approaches that you would like your team to adopt. This type of leadership allows you to know your knowns, anticipate the known unknowns, and be ready to adapt when the unknown unknowns happen! Ensure that these characteristics define your involvement and that you encourage them in all members of your data team.

ALIGNMENT WITH KOTTER'S CHANGE PROCESS

Establishing a data or project team in a school aligns with two of Kotter's eight steps of leading change (see figure 2.1, page 33)—step 2 (build a guiding coalition) and step 4 (enlist a volunteer army; Kotter, n.d.).

Both steps of Kotter's model require a team of people who follow the vision and help lead the change. In step 2, the leader recruits highly effective people who can confidently articulate the vision and views of the data team. In step 4, the people in your data team become your volunteer army that spreads the message of change and advocates for the change to the broader members of the organization (namely, the other teaching staff not involved in the data team). To do this effectively, the data team members need to understand the vision of the leader and the team and the sense of urgency that the change requires, be bought into the change process, and be moving in the same direction as your vision.

By being strategic about the people that you involve in the data team from the beginning, you are setting up conditions later in the change process where the message will travel further, wider, and more effectively.

KEY SUMMARY

- Step 1 requires you to create a data team in your school. A team approach capitalizes on the benefit of having people with different perspectives contribute to the analysis and discussion of the data.

- Establishing a data team fosters true collaboration in your team and approach, rather than leaving one or two people to work on the project in isolation.

- Ensure that your data team meetings have set agendas and plans, are chaired effectively and kept to an appropriate length, and send staff away from the meeting with tasks to collect information and/or share information.

- Have a range of people involved in the data team from all aspects of your school teaching team—senior leaders, middle leaders (curriculum and pastoral), and teachers. Make the contribution voluntary on a year-by-year basis, but be clear about the time commitment required.

- Consider the use of an external consultant or critical friend to support your team either in the initial stages or throughout the change process.

- Prioritize collaboration rather than cooperation. If you ever get to a point where you merely have cooperation, your data team needs a shake-up!

- As the leader, your team will learn from and model the characteristics that you demonstrate--never underestimate the influence you have on their approach! For this reason, demonstrate grit, a growth mindset, and an understanding of the principles of positive psychology to bring out the best in your team.

REFLECTION QUESTIONS

During the process of establishing your data team, use the following questions to reflect on the progress you and your team are making.

BEFORE THE TEAM IS CONSTRUCTED

- Why are you engaging in this process to begin with? What is your purpose?
- Who are some key staff you think should be in your team? How will you invite and encourage staff participation in the data team?
- What meeting structure will you use? Do you need to access any additional resources or support to ensure your meetings are efficient and effective?
- How do you demonstrate grit, positive psychology, and a growth mindset in your own practice? How can you encourage these mindsets in your team from the first meeting?
- How can you improve your transparency around team expectations, goals, logistical details, and so on?
- What are the logistics of your meetings (times, dates, length, frequency, location, required resourcing)?

ONCE THE TEAM IS CONSTRUCTED

- Once you have assembled your team, can you delegate some of the roles to the other members?
- Who will chair the meetings and be the lead on this project?
- What strategies will you use to develop team norms?
- Will you have the team sign and agree to the data assumptions and the team norms?
- Who will be responsible for reading the team norms each meeting (for at least the first six months)?
- As a continuous process, consider the following.
  - How did the meeting go?
  - Are we moving in the direction of the initial aims of the project?
  - Do we need any additional staff or support to maximize the impact?
  - How can we improve the meetings to ensure they are effective and efficient?

chapter four

UNDERSTAND THE DATA AND THE DATA COLLECTION METHODS

Schools are awash with data—I haven't yet come across one that says, "We don't collect enough data." But even though schools collect large quantities of data, they cannot all be used at once, and so leaders need to be able to determine which pieces of data are most relevant or important in achieving the goals of the change project. Therefore, prior to the selection of the most appropriate data for your project, the first step of the data-informed change process requires that the leader and their team understand the type of information and data that they have available in their school.

There is no value in knowing the types of data that are available but having no idea of the purpose, collection method, or meaning of the results. For example, if there is reading comprehension data available for all your students in a percentile result, you and your team need to know what a percentile is. You all need to know what a good, average, and below-average score is. If you have numeracy data that are reported in stanines, every person in your team needs to know what a stanine is and how to use and interpret this information, given what is low, middle, and high. If you have data on reported standardized tests, you need to understand how the data are reported and what the data mean. If your team has multiple data sources that are similar, you all need to understand the nuances in the information that each data set provides. Every data set is different; you need to understand the differences in the data and the data collection methods before you make any decisions based on them.

In my consultancy work, I often work with teachers and school leaders at this initial level to build their understanding of the data. This usually takes the form of working with different data that teachers have access to and helping them understand the meaning and comparability of the numbers. In *Using and Analysing Data in Australian Schools*, I talked about the importance of being able to put a context around numbers, because without context the numbers have no meaning. I particularly like Charles Seife's (2010) statement on this in his book *Proofiness: How You're Being Fooled by the Numbers*:

> For a non-mathematician, numbers are interesting only when they give us information about the world. A number only takes on any significance in everyday life when it tells us how many pounds we've gained since last month or how many dollars it will cost to buy a sandwich or how many weeks are left before our taxes are due . . . We don't care about the properties of the number five. Only when that number becomes attached to a unit—the "pounds" or "dollars" or "weeks" that signify what real-world property the number represents— does it become interesting to a non-mathematician. (p. 9)

As you are the leader in your organization and of your team, I cannot emphasize enough that what you deem to be important and what you talk about regularly will directly influence the culture in your organization or team. Therefore, if you are well versed in the types of data that are being collected in your setting, the difference between the data sets, and what the data mean, your teams will improve their knowledge and buy-in. If you expect your teams to have a good understanding of the data, they will be motivated to learn from you and with you and will follow your lead. If you are skilled in the understanding of the data that are available, you will be able to upskill the members of your team and model the level of understanding that you expect from them. On the other hand, you cannot expect to lead teams through data-informed change if you do not understand the data to begin with. You cannot expect team members to be interested in understanding the data if you are not either. Invest time and effort in learning about the data and always engage in conversations—even difficult ones—with your teams.

AN EXAMPLE OF A PRINCIPAL WHO CHOSE TO LEARN ABOUT THE DATA

At the beginning of the 2017 school year, I led a professional development session on data literacy at an elementary school in southeast Queensland, Australia. The school was in a low socioeconomic catchment area, with literacy results well below other schools in the local area, and literacy and numeracy results below schools in other areas but of a similar demographic. I started the session at the beginning of step 2 of the data-informed change process—I explored the different types of data available, discussed the different reporting standards, demonstrated the comparability (or lack thereof) of the reporting standards, and explained triangulation methods for discerning patterns and trends in the data. While the entire staff engaged and participated in the data literacy session enthusiastically and energetically, I was most impressed by the principal, who, by her own admission, did not have a good understanding of the different types of data that were available.

When teachers were learning to determine what was above average, average, and below average in the student results across a range of assessments, color-coding and triangulating their data, and making sense of the messages and the storytelling in the data sets, the principal participated in all the activities by working with a small group of teachers. She engaged in rigorous discussion with the teachers, supported and assisted them, and asked questions about particular students and particular pieces of data. Although it may have been easier to have not participated or pretended that she had a good understanding of what was going on with the data, this principal demonstrated to everyone in the room that she was learning just like everyone else, and that she valued the exercise. By getting involved in the data literacy activity, she was modeling the approach that she expected of her teachers, and they got this message loud and clear—they were engaged and involved and had great conversations about the progress and achievement of their classes.

As a leader in your school, you need to understand the data and know how they are collected and reported. Although this may be daunting at first (added to which, people in your team might understand it better than you do), embrace the vulnerability and authenticity of not having all the answers, and work collaboratively with your team as you all build your knowledge. If you are not completely sure about a particular type of data, don't be afraid to ask others in your team or your network, or to have others come in to support your team. You and your team must understand data before you can do anything with them.

PRIMING THE ENVIRONMENT BY TALKING ABOUT THE DATA

Earlier in this book, I discussed twelve factors that are important in priming the environment so that the change process is more likely to be successful (see figure 2.3, page 40). One of those elements is *talking about the data*, and this element is particularly important to discuss at this point of the change process.

The most important thing that you can do (if you are the principal) or encourage (if you are a member of the leadership team or middle leadership team) is talk about the data. Leading data-informed change from the middle, or as a single member of a senior leadership team, is difficult and will rarely achieve the best possible results unless all leaders are walking the walk and talking the talk. While I witnessed senior leaders in the United Kingdom doing this regularly, it wasn't until I saw it in Australian schools that I understood the power of the principal (in particular) regularly discussing school data with all members of the school community. As Jen Jackson said at the Data Day Out in 2019, if people want to lead with the data, they need to be fluent in the language and semantics of it—that includes reading, writing, and speaking in data. Not enough leaders are fluent in them, and this is a problem because data literacy is a key barrier to creating a data-informed culture (Tableau Software, 2019).

AN EXAMPLE OF A PRINCIPAL TALKING ABOUT THE DATA

At the end of the 2014 school year, my previous school principal moved on and a new principal—Chris—started at the beginning of 2015. In his opening address during staff week—the first time he spoke to the staff as a group—Chris said, "I am the principal teacher here. I very much see myself still as a teacher, just the principal teacher in this school." That statement resonated with me at the time, and over the following years, he proved that he inherently believed this statement and realized the influence he could, and would, have on curricular and pedagogical change.

During my first year of working with Chris, it became clear that he was passionate about raising the academic rigor in classrooms, raising academic expectations, and improving results. He openly named his goal—to improve the academic outcomes and potential future pathways for students leaving the school—but he also did a few things that I have not seen many principals do to the same extent. Chris was tenacious in pursuing his goal. He spoke about raising expectations—with staff, to parents, and to students—at weekly assemblies, at every parent night, and in many of his newsletter articles. He also invested time and resources into improving results; he created a middle leadership role focused on improvement of student data and performance, funded release time for school data reviews, prioritized spending on an external data coach to support staff, created a data team (which he was *in*) to build momentum, and prioritized time in staff meetings to reflect on and discuss school data. He was walking the talk by modeling the approaches that he hoped teachers in the school would follow. As a result of the way that Chris approached data-informed change in the school, the rest of his leadership team—then the middle leaders, then the teachers—started talking about the goals and the data. I believe it was a key factor in the quite remarkable improvements that we made to student results in a relatively short space of time.

I would like to think that most school leaders are generally good at identifying their priorities, naming goals, and establishing a series of steps to achieve the goals. But what Chris did went well beyond being able to articulate his aspirations—he talked about the goals, the data, and how we were going to improve, at every opportunity. There was nobody in that school community who wouldn't have been able to explain Chris's vision and how he believed we were going to achieve it as a school community. It wasn't just something that he talked about occasionally and then we all forgot about—we couldn't escape it, but in a good way! I cannot emphasize enough the power of him taking the lead, being involved in the process, and reminding people at every opportunity of what we were doing and how we were doing it.

I have learned a lot from Chris, and I encourage other principals that I work with in my consultancy to adopt a similar approach to school improvement and improved results. In 2018, I worked in a similar middle leadership role in a different school, and at every opportunity I asked the principal to come into sessions with students to talk about their data and the importance of the task they were completing. Specifically, I encouraged the principal's involvement in two tasks: (1) a quarterly systemwide writing task and (2) national standardized testing sessions. Although both were cumulative team efforts involving a lot of people in the school, the principal's presence, involvement, and articulation of the school's goals and aspirations for the students prior to them beginning the tasks significantly shifted the students' mood and focus for the better.

After the principal addressed the students, they were more focused and determined to do their best, and they showed pride in their work. In his interactions, the principal encouraged students to work well individually but reminded them that collectively, their results would reflect on us as a school. He emphasized that it was a team game, using collaborative language such as "us" and "we," and motivated students to represent themselves and one another well. It made a remarkable difference! I thanked the principal for contributing, but he actually didn't believe it was all that important for him to talk to students beforehand. I tried to explain the impact he'd had and the students' change in mindset and approach that I had seen from before his speech as compared to after, but he could only see his experience and (what he deemed to be) his small part in the process. But in 2018, these students achieved the best results in the writing task and standardized testing in the school's history. I have no doubt that the principal's presence and involvement in the process played a key role in the improvement in results.

THE LANGUAGE OF DATA DISCUSSIONS

The two leaders that I have just discussed successfully talked about the data by:

- Discussing both progress and achievement measures with staff, students, and the parent body regularly (for staff and students, it was almost weekly)

- Clearly naming their goal and the data that they would be tracking to see whether teachers and students were making progress

- Clearly naming the steps that the community would be taking to achieve the goal

- Regularly speaking about the achievements and growth that they were seeing by acknowledging specific staff and the impact they were having, specific students and their personal achievement or progress, specific classes that had made changes, and cohorts of students who were progressing well; by naming specific staff, students, classes, and year groups, these groups felt proud of their efforts and increased the momentum and motivation for change in others

- Using inclusive language, such as "our students," "us," "our community," "our goals," "we are working toward," and "this is a team effort" to remind all stakeholders of the role they played in the improvement

I have worked with school leaders who tell me that they would like results to improve but who do not regularly talk about the data. Some of these leaders might participate in data discussions or sit on data teams, but they are nervous about naming their goals or are not clear about the ways in which they intend to track progress. It is almost as though they believe that by not naming a goal, they can't possibly fail. But by not naming a goal, a principal and his or her team will never achieve the results they could have.

Failing to name and detail the improvement agenda will also cause leaders to lose their following immediately. How and why could staff be expected to improve when they don't know what they're aiming for? Staff might be prepared to work with and for them to help reach new heights, but without clear guidance and reinforcement of the goals and measuring tools, these key staff will lose interest or motivation—the next thing that comes along that has more attention directed to it will distract them from working with the leader who was too afraid to name their goal or change process.

By clearly and regularly articulating your goals, you immediately give staff a language and a framework that they can work with and around. It provides guidance and structure for the reform efforts and redirects staff if or when they become distracted by other priorities. By referring to the data and your goals regularly, you remind stakeholders about their role in the process, meaning they are less likely to be distracted by other priorities in the first place. Don't underestimate the impact you have when you regularly talk about the data!

ALIGNMENT WITH KOTTER'S CHANGE PROCESS

The regular discussion of data through school improvement efforts relates to two of Kotter's eight steps of leading change (see figure 2.1, page 33)—step 7 (sustain acceleration) and step 8 (institute change; Kotter, n.d.).

Step 7, sustain acceleration, is relevant because it encourages leaders to push through and to lead change with their teams. Indeed, Kotter says, "be relentless when initiating change after change until the vision is a reality" (Kotter, n.d., para. 11). I see Chris's approach to leading change as being relentless—he did not stop talking about our goals to all the relevant stakeholders. As a result, the vision became a reality, and when changes were made and we celebrated success, he raised the bar and relentlessly pursued new goals.

Step 8, institute change, is also relevant because it calls leaders to link the change process and new behaviors to reaching the goal, until the new behaviors become ingrained in the culture of the organization. By regularly discussing the data and talking with staff, teams, students, and parents about the goals, the principal is sustaining acceleration and helping to institute the change. Regularly discussing the data ingrains the data-informed culture in the organization and establishes new behaviors and approaches. This is exactly what Chris did. He celebrated change and recognized staff that were moving out of their comfort zones, trying new things, and moving toward the goal. Over time, these changes were ingrained in the culture, becoming "what we do around here" rather than something new that was being trialed or tested.

As one of the leaders in your school, you need to talk about the data as much as possible. You need to state your goals, let your staff know how you will measure progress, and regularly bring them back to this core goal. You need to invest time and money, where possible, to implement structures that will support your change process. You need to talk to parents about how you are raising standards and what you are doing for their children. You need to write newsletter articles and contact the local newspaper to talk about the changes that are being made and the improvements that will hopefully come (and those you have already witnessed!) as a result. You need to talk to middle leaders and prioritize time in middle leadership meetings to focus on progress toward the goal. You need to talk to students at assembly about the school goals and let them know about the progress that they are making.

If you are a middle leader, your responsibility is twofold: you need to encourage your senior leaders to do these things as much as possible, and in the team in which you are trying to lead change, you need to talk about your goals and the data as much as you can. You need to ask your senior leaders to support your projects and speak to students and parents about the changes you are making. You need to let your senior leaders know about the types of changes that you are making—even if you don't necessarily feel comfortable sharing your work with others—and celebrate the success of the teachers in your teams. No matter where you fit in the leadership hierarchy in your school, use your influence to talk about the change and encourage senior leaders to embrace this approach as well.

LENCIONI'S DYSFUNCTIONS OF A TEAM

In his book *The Five Dysfunctions of a Team*, Patrick Lencioni (2002) narrates a fictional story that outlines five key dysfunctions that affect the way in which teams operate in a business context. The five main issues that lead to dysfunctional teams outlined in Lencioni's work are (1) absence of trust, (2) fear of conflict, (3) lack of commitment, (4) avoidance of accountability, and (5) inattention to results. These five elements are often represented in a triangle to demonstrate the role each element plays. *Absence of trust* represents the wide base of the pyramid, and on top of it falls *fear of conflict, lack of commitment, avoidance of accountability*, and finally *inattention to results* at the very top (Lencioni, 2002).

Lencioni's work is relevant to this discussion on leaders talking about the data, in both the issue of team commitment and inattention to results. Lencioni (2002) states that lack of commitment of team members is a key attribute of dysfunctional teams, and that to prevent this being an issue, there should be clear communication about expectations of team members so they understand the commitment required. If there isn't clear guidance and rigorous team involvement in decision making, team member buy-in is limited. Once the leader and team have decided on the goals or approach, there needs to be appropriate follow-up to hold people accountable for achieving the goals that they decided on. So, by discussing the data and the goals and strategies for tracking improvements, the principal provides the direction that teams require to avoid being dysfunctional.

To prevent the issue of inattention to results, Lencioni (2002) states that goals should be stated clearly and should always be team focused, rather than focused on individuals. If this dysfunction is present in a professional team, team members are more likely to care about their own individual goals rather than the collective goals of the group. Therefore, it is important that the goals or anticipated results of the data team are paramount for the leader, so that members of the team do not believe that they have permission to focus on their own work or goals over the work or goals of the team. By publicly returning to measurable team results and celebrating success whenever possible, this dysfunction can be avoided.

In the context of principals and school leaders leading data-informed change, Lencioni's work highlights the importance of leaders articulating goals that are the focus of the whole team, rather than individuals. If your school community sets out to improve grade 12 results, this responsibility must be shared by the whole grade 12 teaching team and the data team, rather than by one or two teachers attempting to lead change in one area (see the earlier discussion on collective teacher efficacy, page 52). Naming team goals increases individual accountability and ensures that the outcomes reflect on the team rather than on a small group of individuals. This often motivates individuals to work harder for the team, or pull their weight, so that their inattention is not noticed and so results do not reflect poorly on them. It is easy to distance oneself from failed reform efforts if it was someone else's job. As a leader, it is your role to make it everyone's job.

PRIMING THE ENVIRONMENT BY STARTING WITH THE WHY

The second element of priming the environment that is important at this point is the discussion of the *why*. Simon Sinek (2009) is a keen advocate of the power of why—he states that when an organization explains the reasons why they do what they do, rather than what they do or how they do it, they are more successful. Sinek explains that while every organization is able to state what they do, only some can articulate the how, and very few regularly discuss the why.

Although Sinek largely refers to corporate organizations and sales in his work with what he calls the *golden circle* (Sinek, 2009, 2019), I believe this principle is key in leading organizational change and, ultimately, leading data-informed change in schools. Change in schools is constant, and there will always be people who disagree with it. But when staff understand why the change is occurring, it is far easier for them to embrace it and much more likely that they will take a proactive role in the process.

The culture of using data in schools is shifting and evolving at a phenomenal speed. But there are still many people in schools around the world that inherently disagree with collecting and tracking student data, believing that it flies in the face of what education is all about—a holistic education of each and every young person.

While I agree that creativity and interpersonal skills (among other things) can never be assessed by our current standardized testing, we should not discount data all together.

I do think data can and should be used for the right reasons—not to sit higher on success tables, or to outperform a school down the road, but to support students to grow, celebrate success, and maximize the skills and postschooling pathways that students have access to. It is about using data to support the development of literate and numerate global citizens who positively engage with and affect our world in the future. By using data, we know our students better and can cater to their needs more appropriately. That should always be your why.

AN EXAMPLE OF LEADING WITH THE WHY

People who do not agree with the use of data in schools often do not see the bigger picture—usually because they have not been told about it. In 2018, I ran a writing task four times in the same year for grades 7 to 10 students because it was a system requirement. But for me (and for all the staff I engaged in the process), it was also about the importance of improving students' writing ability so they could more effectively engage in society in the future and have a positive impact on the world. This meant that when I spoke with staff about the task, I reminded them why it was important for students to be able to write well. When talking with students, I gave examples of the types of writing they would need to be able to construct when applying for and working in different jobs.

Yes, the system of which we were a part tracked our progress and directed our attention to developing student writing when our literacy results were exceptionally low in 2017. But although the system told us that our data needed to improve and did not clearly link their expectation with the why, we knew exactly why we needed to make these improvements for our students. For us, it was about our students being able to apply for jobs in the future, email their employer, understand paperwork, advocate for their rights and the rights of others, and more. Some research even indicates that literate and numerate citizens have lower crime rates and lower incarceration rates (Houchins, Gagnon, Lane, Lambert, & McCray, 2018). There was no doubt in my mind why students needed to improve their literacy skills.

In the student data and performance role that I served in during 2016, improved grade 12 test results and tertiary ranks meant more options would be available to students, meaning they had more control over their next steps in their life. As tertiary entrance was a top-down system in which places were offered to the highest-achieving students, improved results meant that students were more likely to be accepted into pathways that they were interested in and passionate about. When we spoke with parents, students, teachers, and school leaders, I constantly talked about our why. When our principal spoke to stakeholders, he spoke about the why. It was never about beating other schools or getting the highest number of top scores that the school had ever achieved. It was always about ensuring that each and every individual student, who had his or her own goals and aspirations, was afforded additional postschooling options with improved results.

In both of these examples, reminding staff and students of the why increased buy-in and motivation. So, leading with the why of data and being data informed are key in your leadership of a data-informed community.

FINDING YOUR WHY

During a 2018 presentation to principals and deputy principals in North Queensland, my cofacilitator Catherine Jackson started with an activity about our why that I found interesting. She asked participants the following questions.

- Why is data literacy important to you?
- Why is your answer to question 1 important?
- Why is your answer to question 2 important?
- Why is your answer to question 3 important?
- Why is your answer to question 4 important?
- Why is your answer to question 5 important?
- Why is your answer to question 6 important?

I'd never done this activity before, so I participated too. My responses were:

- Data literacy is important because it helps us learn more about our students' strengths and weaknesses.
- This is important because by knowing more we can cater for our students' needs more effectively.
- This is important because tailored education programs have maximum impact—it also means we are doing our job well.
- This is important because when students achieve and build their self-confidence, they have multiple options available to them when they finish school.
- This is important because it will mean that our students will grow to become adults that can effectively engage with the world, in pathways that interest them and that they enjoy.
- This is important because this is the key role of a teacher.

- This is important because I became a teacher so that I could make a difference.

By doing this simple task, everyone in the room got to his or her core purpose and aims as a teacher by question 5, 6, or 7. Irrespective of where each of us ended up, this activity reminded me that we had all become teachers for similar reasons—to make a positive difference to the next generation. Inherently, we all want our students to succeed and live long, happy, and healthy lives, and ultimately, we want to do everything we possibly can to ensure this occurs. The more often we can remind people of that big picture why, the more likely they are to see the value of the day-to-day tasks such as improving writing scores or improving secondary school exit results. For us, the students we teach and their futures should always be the why.

> *Leadership teams can never really predict how their decision will be accepted. In essence, the most important consideration should be, our "core business"—the students. The why, therefore, has priority as it puts students in front of other priorities.*
> *—Terry O'Connor, former head of campus*

I have worked with leaders who have focused on their why effectively—and often they have had more buy-in from staff. I have also worked with leaders who told their staff that they were doing a particular writing task or standardized testing "because the system says we have to." These efforts have definitely not been as successful as those I've seen from leaders who authentically believe in the purpose and share this with their staff. In a recent interview with Catherine Jackson, an educational consultant and former system and school leader, I asked her about the power of why. She answered:

> *In the absence of a clearly articulated why, people will make one up. So, you leave the why question unanswered at your peril, because people will fill the vacuum. Daniel Pink reminds us that the three things that motivate human activity are autonomy, mastery, and purpose. People need purpose, they need to understand the reasons and the thinking behind what they've been asked to do. The first question that little people ask is why? And that doesn't really change throughout our lives. It's almost a basic human need to put purpose to action. In the absence of articulating the why, people make it up and that could be dangerous. (C. Jackson, personal communication, June 24, 2019)*

Catherine's reference to Daniel Pink is a highly relevant contribution at this point. Articulating the why taps into Pink's (2011) notion of humans being intrinsically motivated at work by three things: (1) autonomy, (2) mastery, and (3) purpose. Pink states that once employees are happy that they are paid fairly for their work, they are motivated by these three elements. Regarding purpose, Pink states that inherently employees want to do work that matters and has a purpose, particularly work that contributes to something larger than themselves. So, by explaining the reasons for decisions we make as leaders, we are reminding teachers of their core reasons for becoming a teacher in the first place and building their sense of purpose and perception of the importance of their role in students' lives.

ALIGNMENT WITH KOTTER'S CHANGE PROCESS

While the power of why has been seen as the brainchild of Simon Sinek in recent years, the idea is not unique. A similar notion is evident in the first step of Kotter's eight-step change process—create a sense of urgency. When leading change, leaders should "help others see the need for change through a bold, aspirational opportunity statement that communicates the importance of acting quickly" (Gupta & Rosenfeldt, 2018). This key first step in Kotter's model asks the people moving through the change process to do exactly what Simon Sinek talks about—communicate their why. Leaders should talk about why the change needs to occur and why it needs to occur immediately. Without this key initial step, it would be almost impossible to continue moving through the series of steps when the team does not understand the relevance or importance of the project in the first place.

KEY SUMMARY

- Step 2 requires you to begin work with your team by learning about the types of data and reporting measures that you have access to in your context.

- By talking about the data, leaders provide a sense of direction for the rest of the staff and the data team.

- Use every opportunity available to talk with your teams and the broader community about the goal you are trying to achieve and your progress toward it. Involve parents, teachers, students, and other middle and senior leaders in this conversation.

- By modeling and leading by example, your team will understand the goal and the steps to achieve it—they are less likely to be distracted by other priorities when they are focused on their collective goal of which they are a part.

- Regular discussion of data and goals ingrains the reform efforts in the school culture, and the new behaviors and processes become part of "what we do around here."

- Starting the data conversation with the why builds a sense of clarity and purpose. Without it, there can be confusion as to the reasons for the change.

- Share the broader picture of the why—not school results or national comparisons but what improvement will mean for your young people. How will improvement affect them and their lives as they move beyond school and become contributing members of society?

- Explain the reasons for the change to your key stakeholders, articulate the goals of your team, and create a sense of urgency about the change.

- Regularly return to the why of what you are doing throughout the change process.

REFLECTION QUESTIONS

During the process of learning about the data, use the following questions to reflect on the progress you and your team are making.

- Do you, and does your team, truly understand the context around the numbers?

- If not, who on staff could assist you with developing this understanding?

- Is there anyone else in your school network or system who could assist in this process?

- What collaborative language can you use to ensure stakeholders see this as everyone's collective responsibility and challenge?

- Do you truly understand progress and achievement measures well enough to discuss both with relevant stakeholders? If not, how can you upskill in this area?

- What is your goal? How can you put it in user-friendly language for each of your stakeholder groups?

- Do you provide tangible examples of progress and growth when you see them? How can you do this better?

- Do you use collective language? How can you embed phrases such as "our students," "us," "our community," "our goals," "we are working toward," and "this is a team effort" more often in your communication?

- How can you share your message and goals with relevant stakeholders? Consider the six stakeholder groups and the six communication options listed in table 4.1. How might you use the communication methods in different ways and with different groups?

Table 4.1: Six Stakeholder Groups and Communication Methods

STAKEHOLDER GROUP	COMMUNICATION METHOD
Students	Assembly address
Teaching staff	Newsletter article
Middle leaders	Social media update
School system	Newspaper article
Parents	Presentation
Broader school community	One-on-one communication

chapter five

SELECT AND COLLECT RELEVANT DATA

No matter the goals of your data analysis or the focus area for your data team, you will never be able to use all the data that are available to you in one analysis or intervention. This is partly due to the huge amounts of data that are generated in and for our schools, but also because it will never all be relevant at the same time. Therefore, the third step in this process is to sort through the excessive amounts of data that you have access to and collect what you need for your analysis.

As Yuval Noah Harari (2016) states in his book *Homo Deus: A Brief History of Tomorrow*, while historically power used to come from accumulating more knowledge, in the 21st century power comes from knowing which data to ignore. Although Harari was speaking more about the vast amounts of data available across a range of fields and broader society, it is absolutely true for the school context. Leaders and teams in schools need to be able to articulate why they are undertaking the review of data in the first place, ascertain which data are important and which are not, and then determine what is most likely to help achieve the school's aspirations and goals as quickly and effectively as possible. By ensuring that you and your newly established team (step 1, see chapter 3, page 45) develop your understanding of the types of data and the collection methods available (step 2, see chapter 4, page 61), you will be ready to make decisions about which data you need in step 3 of this process.

If, for example, your team has identified that numeracy is a particular area requiring review in your setting, then you need to collect the types of data available that report on numeracy performance. You might choose to collect standardized testing results, summative learning area results, or formative weekly quiz results for the class or cohort that you are investigating. Alternatively, if you wanted to review writing progress in your school, you would choose the most appropriate measures that reflect the level of writing of your students—perhaps standardized testing writing results, learning area writing results from English, and formative writing samples from other learning areas. You would probably not include numeracy data in your writing investigation, and you would probably not include writing results in a numeracy analysis. Of course, if you believe a particular data source is relevant, include it. But do not include it for the sake of having more data. Choosing the data that are relevant and useful at this stage will support your analysis and make it easier.

Making incorrect decisions about the types of data you will use at this stage could result in selecting too many sets of data and having too many options or in choosing the wrong data. If you include too many data sets in your analysis, you will get bogged down in the collection and analysis in steps 4 and 5, and you will probably not be able to identify clear trends in the data. For example, if you were analyzing reading progress and chose to use all the literacy data that you had available, it is possible that students' varied results across all aspects of literacy may make it so that you are not able to clearly identify the issues and build your storytelling specifically about reading comprehension. The additional data not specifically related to reading comprehension (such as writing results or learning area results) will distract you from your intended purpose.

TRIANGULATION

I am a firm believer in using triangulation to assist in data analysis—that is, using three or more pieces of data to inform your decision making. Triangulation has historically been used in navigation or research, but it has an important role in using and analyzing school data. If using only one or two types of data, there is a chance that one of the data measures isn't an accurate representation of the student's or cohort's potential. If you were to make decisions based on one or two data sets where one was potentially inaccurate or wrong, then you could possibly form the wrong opinions of a student, class, or cohort, and then initiate processes and changes that do not meet the needs of the learners.

When using three or more pieces of data, the majority of the data guides your analysis (and the subsequent steps that you put in place). If two or more pieces of data tell you something about a student or a cohort, then you believe those two pieces and ignore the third result. If you have four pieces of data, then you trust what the majority of the data (three or four out of the four pieces) is telling you, and so forth. Rosling and colleagues (2018) address the risk of relying on just one piece of data.

> *The most important thing you can do to avoid misjudging something's importance is to avoid lonely numbers. Never, ever leave a number all by itself. Never believe that one number on its own can be meaningful. If you are offered one number, always ask for at least one more. Something to compare it with. (p. 130)*

While Rosling and colleagues weren't talking specifically about school data, their reflections are relevant here. Never believe that single sets of school data or individual numbers by themselves are meaningful without seeing more data first—a student might have been sick on the day, misunderstood the task, or had extensive scaffolding or support to complete the task. Always ask for more data—and prioritize the importance of having at least three types of data so they can be triangulated.

PRIMING THE ENVIRONMENT BY BEING TRANSPARENT

The third key way to prime the environment for data-informed change relates to leaders being transparent with the members of their teams and teachers in their schools. At this stage, and when discussing the types of data to use in your analysis, this is an important consideration.

There will always be times when a leader of a team or organization cannot share information with their team, and when I talk about transparency in this section, I am not referring to those instances. But some leaders choose not to share important information with staff, because of their fear that sharing is unnecessary or could be detrimental to the team. These leaders then justify their decisions by saying things like, "Someone who isn't supposed to see or know the information will find out," or "Staff don't need to know, so I'm not going to tell them." Both of these mindsets reflect little trust in members of their team and are counterproductive to effective data-informed leadership. You need to be open, honest, and transparent as a leader—even more so in the data space, where staff might be concerned about what the data are saying about them.

THE NEW LEADERSHIP PARADIGM

In *Homo Deus: A Brief History of Tomorrow*, Yuval Noah Harari (2016) discusses the notion of knowledge in the 21st century, as well as the old adage *knowledge is power*. Traditionally, this may have been the belief, particularly when organizations used to be heavily dependent on leadership hierarchies and the focus was on management rather than leadership. In the past, the more you knew, the more likely you were to be promoted, and the more successful you potentially would become. Organizational leaders were regularly referred to as bosses, who essentially told staff what they had to do and when they had to do it. But in recent years, organizations have moved away from this model to more horizontal leadership structures, and an emerging priority in a range of employment sectors has been on leadership rather than management.

As Carol Dweck (2008) reports in her book *Mindset: The New Psychology of Success*, "Not . . . everyone will become a leader. Sadly, most managers and even CEOs become bosses, not leaders. They wield power instead of transforming themselves, their workers, and their organization" (p. 74). Unlike in the past, leaders are now people that walk alongside their teams, supporting and developing their staff through collaborative practices. Good leaders now see promotion of their team members as a key indicator of their own success, as it is a reflection of the job they have done in building the capacity of their teams. In the new leadership paradigm, successful and effective leaders show vulnerability and acknowledge openly that they do not have all the answers. Knowing that this shift in leadership has occurred, the *knowledge is power* statement has become redundant, to a certain degree.

But despite a transformation in other realms of educational change and progress, some school leaders and systems still hold on to the perspective of a hierarchical leadership model when thinking about school data. They hide the data, sharing it with a select few, and only when they absolutely have to. But as Harari points out, is it power that we want? Do we want to control the knowledge and have power over our teams? Do we want to prioritize vertical leadership models that promote the power that comes with knowledge? I don't think so. This is no longer the way that organizations are approaching leadership. Good leaders see themselves as participants and learners in the organization, not the people at the top who have all the answers. Knowledge is not power when power is no longer valued as a leadership characteristic.

When I interviewed Wayne Chapman, a current principal in his first year, he stated:

The days of the fearless leader who knows all, makes all decisions, and can do no wrong are long gone (if they ever really existed). Schools are highly complex and complicated organizations that require teams of leaders operating in multiple directions across differing and often pressing timelines. (W. Chapman, personal communication, June 19, 2019)

His response is a great example of the new paradigm of leadership.

If we want to work alongside our teams as 21st century educational leaders, we need to hand over sole knowledge of school data to them. Leaders can no longer be the gatekeepers of information, only allowing a select few into the data conversation—they need to be transparent with this information wherever and whenever possible.

DIFFERENT APPROACHES TO DATA TRANSPARENCY

Having taught in both Australia and the United Kingdom, I have witnessed the vast differences between systems with respect to data and league tables, and the way in which data are discussed and shared with staff and students. The discussion of data in the UK is far more frequent and transparent than that which I have seen in Australia. Where teachers in the UK are shown class data, school data, and sometimes value-added data attributed to specific teachers, many leaders and schools in Australia maintain that data should be released to staff only on a need-to-know basis. I experienced a key moment early on in my data-informed journey while teaching in the UK, when I saw that every grade 9 student, from top to bottom, had his or her science learning area results listed on a permanent bulletin board in the hall outside the science lab. Having been educated and trained as a teacher in Australia, this transparency of results was confronting, and I still cannot believe that it was the norm in the UK as recently as the 2000s.

But there are always two sides to every story, and while initially I found that level of transparency surprising and questioned its value, I also realized that my students were collectively more articulate about their performance, targets, and strategies for improvement than any of my previous students (and indeed any of my students since). My students in the UK could tell me their target grade for each learning area they studied, the grade they were currently achieving, and the things they needed to do to attain their target grade. In a range of schools I have visited since I returned from the UK, fear of the wrong people seeing the information has dominated conversations regarding data transparency.

In a recent interview with principal Chris Mayes, he gave an example of the way in which his previous schools approached data:

> *I've previously come from schools where data is pretty free and common, except it was only used by a certain group, and that was usually the college leadership team. It was wheeled out to staff at the beginning of the year to tell everyone how well we'd done (or otherwise), and that was it. Subject heads of curriculum were given big books of data, and I'd dare say, they'd get filed away pretty quickly. Certainly, when you would talk to teachers about what they knew about the data, it was usually very little. If you're going to have data that's going to be a part of what goes on in the classroom, the people in the classroom have got to be the ones that actually are a part of having an input into what it is and what we want to do.*
> *(C. Mayes, personal communication, June 11, 2019)*

AN EXAMPLE OF THE POWER OF TRANSPARENCY

In 2016, I was working with students and teachers to improve results in the grade 12 Queensland Core Skills (QCS) Test (which affects tertiary entrance ranks). I had some success in the United Kingdom with predicting results in the final tests for students based on their performance in the practice tests, and so I began to do so with my Australian students. As a key predictor of the school mean of the test was the proportion of students who achieved As and Bs over Cs and Ds, I thought it logical to predict how the students were going in their practice tests on an A to E scale. This would provide me with an idea of how they were progressing and enable me to give feedback on whether they were either on track, at risk, or traveling well.

After the first set of practice test results came back, I generated estimated grades for every student doing the tests in grade 12 from A to E. Given my work in my doctoral thesis on feedback and my experience with transparency of results in the United Kingdom, I knew that I needed to close the feedback loop for the data to have the greatest impact. I thought about ways in which I could share this information with students, and I set out to arrange a plan with my principal at the time, Chris. But when I approached him a few days later, he asked me not to share the data with students, as he was worried how the D-grade students would take the news.

While I understood his concerns, I was disappointed. Students in my doctoral study desperately wanted to know as much information about their performance as possible, and I knew there were students in the grade 12 cohort who wanted to know how they were tracking as well. Having invested many years of work into researching feedback, I felt it was useless for that information to sit on my laptop and never be shared with students. If a student achieved a D in the test at the end of the year, it would affect not only them but also their peers. Because of this, I felt it was better to have the conversation with them when we could do something about it rather than waiting until it was too late to fix.

I was trying to work out how best to approach this with Chris a second time, so that we could come up with a compromise on how I could use the data in feedback with students, when I was approached by the school captain, Zach. He had found out that I was working with predicted grades for each of the grade 12 tests and overall grades and asked to see them. I explained that I wasn't meant to show him, but his persistence and my belief in the power of feedback (and my occasional disregard of rules when I believe it is for the right reasons) saw us agree to meet in a classroom beside the teachers' lounge at lunchtime to show him where I thought he was at with the practice exams.

When I arrived at the room, I saw that Zach had brought a few friends with him. I was already apprehensive about sharing the data with Zach, and even more so about sharing it with multiple students. But I felt as though I was doing this for the right reasons, and so we sat down and I showed them what I had been working on. Because the spreadsheet contained a lot of data, the students asked if I could project it on the whiteboard. I thought, why not?

As I walked them through the different tests and estimated grades, a few more grade 12 students came in. As I talked about the percentage of students overall that were predicted As, Bs, Cs, and Ds, even more students came in. I quickly worked out that Zach had told quite a few of his peers what I was doing, and that about twenty-five of them had decided to come along to see what grade they were working at.

While I was apprehensive about sharing information that I had explicitly been asked not to share, the conversation was engaging and positive. The boys were talking about the strengths of the group, areas for individual growth, and ways that they could motivate others to improve. In the middle of this extraordinary conversation about how to get the grade 12 cohort working harder together, Chris walked in. My heart sank immediately, and I wondered just how much trouble I would be in. Chris stood at the back of the room for about ten minutes, contributing a little to the discussion on improvement but mostly observing what was happening before quietly leaving.

After lunch, I asked a friend on staff for some advice—should I find Chris and apologize? Should I wait until he brought it up? They reminded me of the words of Rear Admiral Grace Hopper: sometimes it is easier to ask for forgiveness than get permission. So, I resolved to apologize profusely and beg for forgiveness when Chris inevitably called me in. That afternoon, I walked straight past Chris while going to my car. He said goodbye and waved me off as if I had not completely ignored his instructions. And he never mentioned it!

Over the next few weeks, and through working with the dean of teaching and learning, I was allowed to share the predictions with the entire grade 12 cohort. I surmised that they had heard the conversations that the other students were having and had begun to see the value in transparency of the data. I eventually got to the point where I was able to have conversations with the entire cohort about how many As, Bs, Cs, and Ds we were tracking toward and ways that we could improve together.

Although I am a big advocate of feedback and discussing results with students, I could never have anticipated the exceptionally positive way in which the students received these predictions. They increased motivation, a sense of comradery, and teamwork, and they helped students set goals for the tests. They wanted to improve their results and move up the five-point scale to benefit themselves and their peers for their tertiary entrance rankings. To this day, Chris and I have never had a conversation about me sharing the data after he told me not to—I guess this is my chance to say, "Sorry, Chris!"

Although I did not do the "right" thing in this instance, transparency and the discussion with students about their results were where the true power lay in this data. Once students knew what they were predicted to achieve and decided they weren't happy with the result, they worked exceptionally hard to improve. Student leaders in the school began to speak to their peers about the results, supported and encouraged one another, and had genuine conversations about the things that made a difference—question difficulty, easy wins for marks, average scores, and attendance at practice sessions.

The tertiary entrance ranks that were released at the end of that academic year were the highest for that cohort in the school's history, and I have no doubt it was because of the feedback. Because of the high results, many students were offered places in tertiary courses that were on their wish list, but that they never thought their entrance score would be high enough to get into. Transparency of the data and feeding back to students were key to this success.

DATA DEMOCRATIZATION

Although the preceding example concerns transparency of data with students, transparency with data also relates to the way in which you share data and tracking methods with the teachers in your learning community.

In the business context, widening the access to data has been termed *data democratization*, or third-generation business intelligence and analytics (Fleming et al., 2019). This concept has existed in other industries for a few years, but it is just as applicable in the education sector as it is elsewhere. Historically, the first generation of business intelligence and analytics was the introduction and use of information technology (IT), and an IT team in organizations. The second generation introduced the notion of decentralized access to information—as more people in the organization became involved in business intelligence and analytics, more than just the IT team had access to information. We are currently in the third generation—one of data democratization (Fisher & Good, 2019).

Fisher and Good (2019) state that data democratization is:

- Democratization itself (all the data are in one place and accessible to all staff)
- Augmented intelligence (organizations work on raising data literacy of their employees by using technology)
- Embedded everywhere (as in using data is no longer a destination that we are working toward; it is at the heart of the business)

In a data democracy, more people in the organization are empowered to have access to and use the data, rather than a few key staff, and data are freed in a responsible way—the right data are available to the right people at the right time in a trusted manner. As a result of the data democracy, more users are able to ask questions of the data, which creates more opportunities to address business problems. While trust is still a key issue in data democratization, like money, data are deemed to be an asset of the organization.

But transparency is sometimes harder to embrace than it sounds. I have worked with a number of principals who disagree with the use of data walls, despite the fact that they are identified as a high-yield strategy in raising student achievement (Sharratt & Fullan, 2012). I have seen data walls that have not been built, or not been moved to a more appropriate place for fear of "the wrong person seeing that personal information," or that "someone might happen to walk through the building at night and accidentally see it," or (my personal favorite) "Parents and Friends meetings are being held in this room, and they might see the data."

Rather than finding excuses why data should *not* be shared with your teaching teams, think of ways in which you can share data while minimizing risk. Rather than thinking that no school data should be shared with staff and only drip-feeding small bits when necessary, aspire to build a data democracy where you share all school data and then choose the parts that you will not. Do not wait until things get so bad that you have to set up a data team, employ more staff, or engage an external consultant to fix the problem. Talk about the data, talk about the challenges, talk about the things that didn't go to plan—just talk about it!

You cannot expect your team to work toward improvement if they are not sure how or cannot see their improvement along the way. You also cannot expect them to work with you and buy into your vision for change if they cannot see the need for the change, or if they feel like they are being kept from some of the information. Don't give them half the picture—increase their buy-in by being open and transparent from the start. Lead a data democracy!

KEY SUMMARY

- Step 3 requires you and your team to select and collect the data that you need to inform your project or area of investigation.

- Transparency with the data is key as it leads to openness and clarity rather than obscurity and ambiguity.

- Sharing data with staff teams shows that you trust your teams and want to work with them toward improvement.

- Share as much of the data as you can—with students, project teams, and the whole staff.

- Focus on the benefits of sharing student data and opening up improvement conversations rather than reasons that it could be an issue.

- We are in the third generation of business intelligence and analytics—lead a data democracy!

- Flip your approach on its head! Resolve to share all the data and pull back the few small pieces you should not share, rather than only sharing small pieces when you think it is necessary.

REFLECTION QUESTIONS

During the process of sorting and selecting the data that are useful for your analysis, use the following questions to reflect on the progress that you and your team are making.

- What data sources are available in your school?

- Go back to your core purpose—why are you undertaking this process in the first place? What data will authentically and honestly provide you with information about the focus of your investigation?

- What are your views on the transparency of data?

- Do you see yourself leading a data democracy? Why or why not?

- Is your school in the third generation of business intelligence? Why or why not? What can you do to shift your organization along in this space?

- What else can you do to increase the transparency of data with your teaching team and with your students?

chapter six

DISPLAY RELEVANT DATA IN AN APPROPRIATE FORMAT

Displaying and ordering your data in a user-friendly format support your analysis. If you are dealing with large cohorts of students and three or more data sets, you need to find a way of organizing the data in a way that is not overwhelming and so that your teams can decipher trends in subsequent steps of the change process. Unfortunately, this process is time consuming—reports indicate that organizing the data can take up to 80 percent of the time spent in analysis efforts (Jones & Pickett, 2019)!

SHADE OR COLOR-CODE THE DATA

In the previous chapter, I talked about the importance of triangulating data so that you have three or more data sets to analyze. Once these sets of data are in the same place, the next step should be shading or color-coding the data to assist with your analysis. Color-coding data as green (above average), yellow (average), and red (below average)—or shading the data as white, light grey, and dark grey—is one way to identify trends. For example, the data for the four students in table 6.1 (page 90) have not yet been color-coded, but with an understanding of the context around the numbers, it is possible to scan through the results to see that Rashad is performing well, Kate is finding English and reading difficult, and Tim and Linh have some varied results.

89

Table 6.1: Sample Data Set for Four Students

Student name	End of semester English learning area result	Standardized testing—Reading	External assessment—Reading comprehension
Tim	C	85th percentile	Stanine 9
Kate	D+	42nd percentile	Stanine 2
Linh	A	75th percentile	Stanine 6
Rashad	A-	93rd percentile	Stanine 8

But discerning these trends requires a good understanding of the meaning of the values, and it takes time to determine trends in data. This table also only presents three sets of data for four students—in reality, we will be looking at a lot more data! But if we shade or color-code the data, we can capitalize on the superiority of visuals (Ezard, 2015; Jackson & Jackson, 2018; Tableau Software, 2019), and the trends become more immediately identifiable. Notice the significant difference between table 6.1 and table 6.2. (Visit **go.SolutionTree.com/leadership** to view a color-coded version of this table, with green representing As, yellow representing Bs and Cs, and red representing Ds or lower.)

As Jen Jackson stated at the Data Day Out Sydney in May 2019, text alone has a 10 percent recall rate, images have a 65 percent recall rate, and visuals with color have an 82 percent recall rate (Tableau Software, 2019). I think the preceding example illustrates just how powerful a shaded visual is when compared to one that contains solely text. The addition of red, green, and yellow color, viewable at **go.SolutionTree .com/leadership**, is even more impactful. As well as it being quicker and easier to interpret trends when we utilize the power of visuals and visuals with color, it also helps us to remember the results. As Jackson and Jackson (2018) suggest:

> *Visualizing content improves our connection to the content. It attracts our eyes, ensnares our minds and stays lodged in our memory long afterwards. It can make even the blandest data infinitely more palatable. Oh yes, when we push beyond the comfortable familiarity of words and visualize the content, the results can be quite thrilling. (p. 42)*

Using the principles of triangulation, it would appear that Tim is of above-average ability but has not performed to the best of his ability in English, whereas Linh has

Table 6.2: Sample Shaded Data Set for Four Students

Student name	End of semester English learning area result	Standardized testing—Reading	External assessment—Reading comprehension
Tim	C	85th percentile	Stanine 9
Kate	D+	42nd percentile	Stanine 2
Linh	A	75th percentile	Stanine 6
Rashad	A-	93rd percentile	Stanine 8

performed better in English than in standardized testing, meaning she has more average results overall than above average. Kate finds English and reading comprehension difficult, but Rashad is a high-performing student who has excellent results across all three assessments.

If shading or color-coding data is the approach you decide to take, use conditional formatting in your spreadsheeting program to automatically shade or color-code the data for you. The easiest way to do this is to decide the cutoffs that you are happy to consider average results, and color these yellow (or shade them light grey). Anything above the top score in the average bracket should be colored green (or shaded white), and anything below the lowest score should be colored red (or shaded dark grey).

OTHER DISPLAYS OF DATA

As an alternative to color-coding or shading, you might choose to use column graphs, tables of results, or percentages of students at each level to represent and display your data. You may also have a learning management system (LMS) that produces visual representations or data reports for you, either in column graphs or longitudinal movement of results. But be discerning—consider how the data need to be represented to provide you with the information that you require. If the LMS-generated reports serve your purpose, then use them. If they do not, work with your team to develop other ways of representing the data that are more conducive to your goals.

Whichever way you and your team decide to represent the data, be mindful of the fact that the way in which you display them will influence the following steps in this change process. Different methods can identify different strengths and weaknesses in the data. So, where possible, use multiple data sets and multiple representations to prevent misinterpretation of the data in the storytelling stage.

THE ROLE OF TECHNOLOGY IN SCHOOL DATA USE

The role of technology in conducting analyses is a common factor in the discussion about data use in schools. In his book *Homo Deus: A Brief History of Tomorrow*, Yuval Noah Harari (2016) discusses the increase in work that machines do for humans, as well as the challenge of maximizing their impact and putting them to good use while recognizing the things that they will never be able to do. In his discussion, Harari talks about the decoupling of intelligence and consciousness. Nonconscious, but highly intelligent, machines are increasingly required to do the work of humans—be it self-driving cars, automated checkouts in supermarkets, or, in our context, LMSs that track student data and progress.

The benefit is that these smart machines save us time and effort, meaning more of them are built as more jobs and processes in society are replaced by smart machines. But we have only mastered the creation of intelligent machines—we have not created machines that can replicate consciousness and replace humans. Although Harari discusses the notion of smart machines that are learning to build their own consciousness, he asks, Can or will they ever truly be able to do the things that humans do? In other words, will artificial intelligence (AI) ever be able to do the data storytelling for us?

One positive way that technology supports the use of data in schools is in the representation of data. Technology makes our job of analysis and visualization so much easier and more automatic. Long gone are the days of ruling up straight lines and manually coloring tables and graphs of our data, or pages of quiz results and test grades in the back of the teacher diary where trends may or may not have been easily identifiable. Technology has given us the ability to quickly and easily organize, collate, and display data, but technology and AI will never be able to do the storytelling for us.

In the conversation about using data in schools, there is no end to the number of LMSs, tracking websites, and analysis software applications that schools can buy or build to help with the use, analysis, and visualization of data. And while these applications, and the automation they provide, do make our jobs easier in some ways, they are unable to do the most important task—that is, combine the intelligence and understanding of the data with the consciousness of people and context. Using our knowledge of the context and students in conjunction with our understanding of their data should always be our priority.

USING TECHNOLOGY ALONGSIDE OUR UNDERSTANDING OF STUDENTS

In one of my first consulting presentations, a principal asked why we were spending time triangulating, analyzing, and discussing trends in data when technology and AI could potentially do the work for us in the future. I responded by saying that while I agreed machines can sort, color-code, and graph our data for us to some extent, it is our knowledge of students and contexts that brings the data to life. As Harari (2016) says, intelligence and consciousness have been decoupled; machines excel at intelligent work, not conscious work. When it comes to schools, machines will never be able to replicate the complex understanding of our students that teachers bring to the data.

How could machines ever understand home environments, student issues, areas of passion and innovation, stories of creativity and enthusiasm, and other areas of strength in our students that assessments don't measure? As reported in the *Economist*, "Although AI systems are impressive, they can perform only very specific tasks: a general AI capable of outwitting its human creators remains a distant and uncertain prospect" ("Artificial Intelligence: March of the Machines," 2016). I believe we will always rely on our own consciousness (in conjunction with technology) to complete the full data cycle and do the storytelling. By all means, capitalize on the intelligence of technology, but remember that it isn't just about the numbers. Technology is just one part of the narrative (Pringle, 2019).

THE IMPACT OF YOUR VIEWS ON YOUR STAFF'S PERSPECTIVES

As a leader of data-informed change in your school, you need to consider the emphasis you place on knowing and understanding the data *and* on the importance of experience and an understanding of context. Not only do you need to have a good understanding of how you view these two elements of data-informed leadership working together, but you also need to be able to articulate this to your teams. If you are able to articulate the importance of combining anecdotal and qualitative data alongside quantitative data to improve the storytelling, you reinforce the power of relationships and the importance of knowing students. Teachers generally join the profession because they want to help young people—if you, as the leader, focus only on the numbers, you risk removing the human element that attracted most teachers to this work in the first place.

Data skeptics will focus on the machine aspect of data analysis and visualization and be happy to blame the process of focusing on numbers instead of students if things go wrong. But if you promote the use of data and the importance of being data informed alongside the need for a contextual understanding of the individuals, then you are showing teachers that you recognize the value of their experience and perspectives and that you are not reducing the students to numbers. As Jackson and Jackson (2018) say in *How to Speak Human*:

> An age of robots and AI-driven efficiency lies ahead of us, friends. But this doesn't mean we need to start speaking android. The new roles that will inevitably emerge will be more dependent on our relationships with each other. Yes, our work will continue to rely on humans. Creatures comprising 60 percent water and 40 percent unfathomable thought processes, unreasonable behaviors, and unpredictable emotions. Filled with all sorts of psychological and physiological inconveniences. Capable of equal parts frustration and absolute delight. (pp. xx–xi)

Similarly, the *Economist* ("Artificial Intelligence: March of the Machines," 2016) reports that AI will never be able to do work that calls for empathy and human interaction. So, we need the beautiful complexity of ourselves and our understanding of our students to be effective data storytellers.

KEY SUMMARY

- Step 4 requires you to display the data that you will be using in a format that is user friendly.

- Triangulate the data that you are using—don't begin an analysis with one or two data sets. Three pieces of data (or more) ensure inaccurate data can be identified and ignored.

- When triangulating the data, use a shading or color-coding system such as red (below average), yellow (average), and green (above average) to support your analysis. Shading or color-coding allows you to quickly and easily identify trends in the data.

- Use the majority of your shaded or color-coded data to inform your ideas on the performance of students or the cohort.

- Utilize other displays of data that will support your analysis—consider column graphs, longitudinal line graphs, or box plots.

- Technology is your friend in the analysis—utilize the power of automation and conditional formatting to develop your data representations.

- Technology can do the intelligent work for us, but it will never be able to do the conscious work. Capitalize on technology, but use it in conjunction with your understanding of your students and the context to inform decision making.

REFLECTION QUESTIONS

During the process of organizing the display of your data, use the following questions to reflect on the progress that you and your team are making.

- Are you using shading or color-coding to its full capacity?

- Are you able to identify the trends in shaded or color-coded data? If not, why? Do you need someone to help you with this? If so, who is the best person to support you?

- Are you using triangulated data to inform your decision making? What else do you need to know about triangulation?

- Is your team utilizing shaded or color-coded data in conjunction with their understanding of students to inform their decision making?

- What other data displays do you need?

- Do the displays that you have represent the information in the way that you need? If not, why not? What can you do to ensure the data are representing the information you're after in a way that is useful and user friendly?

- Are you communicating with your staff that they should be using their understanding of the data in conjunction with their understanding of students?

- How can you make it more explicit that teachers need to combine the data with their understanding of the students? Can you provide examples to your staff on how to do this?

chapter seven

ANALYZE THE DATA AND IDENTIFY TRENDS

As a leader you need to find ways to provide people with the time to process data and explore interpretations and implications. You need to ensure that people actually understand the data set of the visualization/representation that is being shared. It is easy to overestimate teachers' capacity within this type of knowledge. It is important to provide them with the time and space to process this information via inquiry questions or walk them through some kind of process to make meaning of the data. The real challenge is to make the time to do this properly and to ensure that people have the capacity to move from a rudimentary

Once the data have been prepared in the reports or formats required, you and your team need to look for trends or stories in the data. Some might be immediately identifiable, while others will require your team to sit with the data for longer and employ your curiosity and growth mindsets. The answers won't necessarily jump out at you—do not stop when you have one or two thoughts or ideas about the data. If the analysis of the data and trends was that easy, then you probably would not have needed to do it with a team of people in the first place!

This step is a good opportunity to schedule time for you and your data team to analyze the data for an extended period. Sit with the data and bounce ideas off one another; learn

> *understanding to a more in-depth one. An integral part of achieving this is providing the time for people to process the information, express divergent views, and address these views.*
> —Wayne Chapman, principal

from the different perspectives in your team; and encourage team members to brainstorm and identify new challenges and areas of growth. Push them to think outside the box and consider the issue from a range of perspectives in an objective manner. Ask what questions they have, or what they notice and wonder about the data. Show your vulnerability by exploring the data and learning with them. Demonstrate the professional trust that you have in them by valuing their contributions and expressing appreciation for their involvement.

QUESTIONS TO SUPPORT DATA CONVERSATIONS

If the conversation about data does not come easily, support your team with guiding questions. A common approach to analyzing data in schools is to "notice" and "wonder" what the data are saying. While these questions do offer a starting point, we must move past superficial questions to ones that provide in-depth analysis and problem-solving strategies, such as:

- What do you notice about the data? What are they telling you?
- What do you wonder about the data?
- What are they measuring? Are they reliable? When were the data collected? Who collected the data? What is the purpose?
- What questions do you have about the data? Whom do you need to approach to answer these questions?
- What do the data tell you about student achievement?
- What do the data tell you about student progress?
- Who are the outliers and why? Why do these anomalies exist?
- Are there any data that don't make sense? Why don't they make sense?
- Are there any immediately identifiable trends in the data? How do you know they are trends?
- Which individuals or groups have performed well? What is most remarkable about the data? How do you know they performed well (what evidence is there)?
- What areas of the data can you celebrate?

- Which individuals or groups have performed poorly? What areas need your attention? How do you know they performed poorly (what evidence is there)?

- Is there anything noteworthy about the "middle group" of students? Do the data indicate that they require additional support or guidance? How do you know this?

- Are the data similar to previous results? Or do they show an improvement or a decline? What does this tell you about school programs, the approach, or the cohort? Are longitudinal comparisons available?

- What are some possible reasons for the results?

- What do the data tell you about school programs or approaches? How do you know this is a reflection of the school programs or approaches (what evidence is there)?

- What specifically needs to change as a result of the data? How can the data inform teaching? What are the next steps? Why does it need to change? Who will benefit from the change? What specifically will you do to make this change? What is the timeline for this change? What will you do if there is no improvement in the future? When will you measure these data again? How will you know that this change has been successful?

- What do the data tell you?

- What do the data not tell you?

- How can you use these data to celebrate success or achievement with students?

- How can you use these data in feedback for and with students?

Select a few questions from this list to support your analysis and discussion—it is not intended to be a list that you and your team will work through from start to finish. Choose the questions that are most relevant or that you believe could be most useful and use them to guide and prompt your conversation.

ANALYSIS TEMPLATES

If your team requires further assistance with this process, one of the following templates may assist you. The four templates shown here are designed to support your analysis and probe some of the important learnings in the data to enable effective change. A completed example and reproducible version of each can be found in the appendix (page 177).

Figure 7.1 (page 100) is a way of considering three sets of data that you have available, and features questions that might arise from the data. If you have triangulated and color-coded the data as above average, average, and below average, this template allows you to compare the percentage of students that sit in each of these categories for these assessments.

Group:			Focus area:		
Assessment 1			**Assessment 2**		
% of students below average	% of students at the average	% of students above average	% of students below average	% of students at the average	% of students above average

Assessment 3			Things I notice about the data:		
% of students below average	% of students at the average	% of students above average			

Things I wonder about the data:	Questions I have about the data:

Specific steps for modifying teaching/programs/approaches:

Figure 7.1: Template 1 for considering three sets of data.

Figure 7.2 encourages the user to consider both areas of strength that are identifiable in the data and areas that require further attention or focus. This template offers a summary of the issues in the data and the areas that should be celebrated. It provides additional depth to the analysis as it asks slightly different questions than Template 1.

Guiding questions	Response
What is the particular area of interest (for example, grade 5 literacy)?	
What trends do you immediately notice in the data?	
Identify three areas of strength in the data.	1. 2. 3.
What does each of the strengths tell you about your programs, strategies, or teaching and learning?	1. 2. 3.
How can you celebrate the areas of strength?	1. 2. 3.
Identify three areas of concern in the data.	1. 2. 3.
What does each of the areas of concern tell you about your programs, strategies, or teaching and learning?	1. 2. 3.
How can you address or make changes to improve the areas of concern?	1. 2. 3.

Figure 7.2: Template 2 to consider areas of strength and areas in need of further attention in the data.

Figure 7.3 (page 102) is of most use if your team is looking specifically for areas of strength or areas that are progressing well. It encourages the user to expand on the questions in figure 7.2 that focus on the positive news stories and unpacks those positives to ensure the learning is transferred to other areas in the school community.

Guiding questions	Response
What is the particular focus area (for example, grade 9 attendance)?	
What positive trends are immediately identifiable in the data?	
What are three bright spots in the data?	1. 2. 3.
Why is each of these things a bright spot?	1. 2. 3.
Which element of your school program or approaches has led to the bright spots?	1. 2. 3.
How can you celebrate these bright spots?	1. 2. 3.
What learning is there from these bright spots for other areas of the school?	1. 2. 3.

Figure 7.3: Template 3 to unpack the positives in the data.

Figure 7.4 is the most challenging to complete, as it asks the user to focus on the negative trends that are occurring in the data. The goal of this template (and the others) is that it will lead to measurable change in your school, so being up front about what the data are saying is an important first step. Some of the questions might be difficult to answer, but that means they are questions that need to be asked.

Guiding questions	Response
What is the particular focus area (for example, grade 2 reading)?	
What are the immediately identifiable trends in the data?	
What are the three most significant areas of concern? (List from most pressing to least pressing.)	1. 2. 3.
Why is each of these areas concerning?	1. 2. 3.
What does each of these areas of concern tell you about your programs, strategies, or learning and teaching?	1. 2. 3.
How can you address each of the areas of concern (what changes, strategies, or approaches could you use to address these concerns)?	1. 2. 3.
Do these areas of weakness affect or reflect any other areas of your school programs or approaches?	1. 2. 3.

Figure 7.4: Template 4 to unpack the areas of concern in the data.

ANALYZING SETS OF DATA

One method of analyzing your data set is presented in figure 7.5 (page 104).

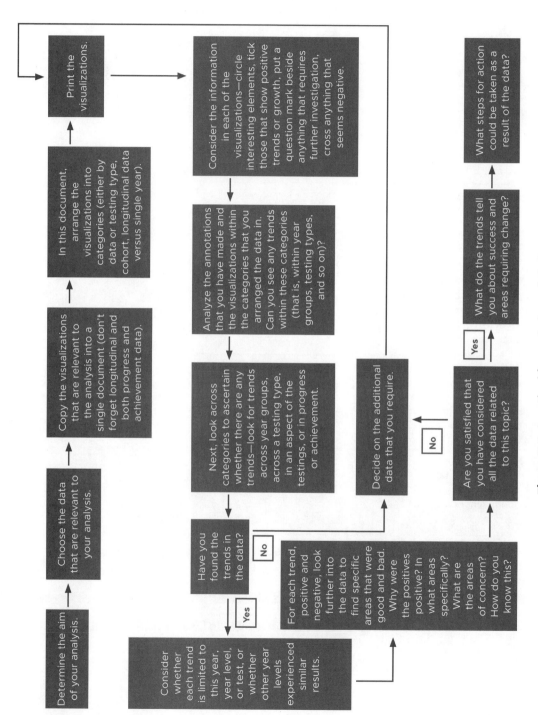

Figure 7.5: A method for analyzing a data set.

If you are presented with many different visualizations or need to consider data across a number of areas (year levels, learning areas, or testing types), you may find it easier to print the visualizations in the categories that you intend to perform your first level of analysis on. For example, in a recent data review of standardized testing for a school in Victoria, Australia, I grouped and printed the visualizations in the categories illustrated in figure 7.6.

Standardized testing analysis			
GRADE 3 DATA	GRADE 5 DATA	GRADE 7 DATA	GRADE 9 DATA
Current year reading results	Current year reading results	Current year reading results	Current year reading results
Current year writing results	Current year writing results	Current year writing results	Current year writing results
Current year numeracy results	Current year numeracy results	Current year numeracy results	Current year numeracy results
Longitudinal reading results	Longitudinal reading results	Longitudinal reading results	Longitudinal reading results
Longitudinal writing results	Longitudinal writing results	Longitudinal writing results	Longitudinal writing results
Longitudinal numeracy results	Longitudinal numeracy results	Longitudinal numeracy results	Longitudinal numeracy results

Figure 7.6: Grouping of data in a review of standardized testing.

By moving down through the data within these four year-level categories and completing my first set of annotations (as positives, areas of concern, and points of interest), I quickly began to see trends emerge. The grade 3 students were particularly strong across all three testing areas in the current year and had the highest results in recent history. The grade 7 students performed the lowest across all three tests and achieved some of the lowest results in the school's history. Generally, the grade 7 students' results had declined over the last three to four years. The grade 5 and grade 9 students' testing results were quite varied with no clear pattern in their longitudinal data.

Following my analysis within these categories, I considered the data in a second manner: the testing area across year-level categories (see figure 7.7, page 106).

Instead of looking for trends in the annotations down through categories as I did in the first analysis, I considered the annotations and trends across the testing areas. I could see that numeracy was a strength across the school—every year level was higher compared to state averages than they were in other tests, and numeracy was the test in which students generally achieved the highest averages overall. Further, writing

Standardized testing analysis			
GRADE 3 DATA	GRADE 5 DATA	GRADE 7 DATA	GRADE 9 DATA
Current year reading results	Current year reading results	Current year reading results	Current year reading results
Current year writing results	Current year writing results	Current year writing results	Current year writing results
Current year numeracy results	Current year numeracy results	Current year numeracy results	Current year numeracy results
Longitudinal reading results	Longitudinal reading results	Longitudinal reading results	Longitudinal reading results
Longitudinal writing results	Longitudinal writing results	Longitudinal writing results	Longitudinal writing results
Longitudinal numeracy results	Longitudinal numeracy results	Longitudinal numeracy results	Longitudinal numeracy results

Figure 7.7: Grouping of data in a review of standardized testing.

was a consistent area of concern—these were the only visualizations in which there were results below the state averages. In addition, the writing results seemed to be declining in every year level.

Of course, further analysis can take place following these initial processes of looking down and across the categories. In this instance, I began to look at and compare the position of student averages from two years prior and their distance above the state averages to the current year. I also looked at each test in each year level and did further analysis of whether writing criteria issues were similar from year to year. It is important to consider the ways in which you can look down, across, and through different categories of the data.

Ultimately, the process of analyzing the data to identify trends relies heavily on you considering alternate viewpoints and finding things that you were not necessarily looking for in the first place. It requires you and your team to embrace vulnerability and admit to not have all the answers. Get into the data with your team and be a part of the process. Show your team members that this is your priority by being there and participating in the conversations. Remember, model the behavior and approaches that you would like your team to adopt. Don't sit on the sidelines.

You will know you are coming to the completion of step 5 when you have a list of key trends from the data. You should summarize the trends as in figure 7.8.

The trends identified in the data set are:

1.

2.

3.

4.

5.

6.

7.

8.

Figure 7.8: List of trends.

The final step before moving on to step 6 is to prioritize the significance of the trends you have identified. To do this, you and your team should rewrite the list of trends from what you perceive as the most pressing issue at the top through to the least pressing. Set aside a good amount of time with your team to have this conversation and make decisions about the position of each trend. Remember, capitalize on the different perspectives of your team and make these decisions together. Ensure that you have the trends ordered and numbered by the end of this conversation.

PRIMING THE ENVIRONMENT BY EMBRACING THE POWER OF VULNERABILITY

> *We desperately need more leaders who are committed to courageous, wholehearted leadership and who are self-aware enough to lead for their hearts, rather than unevolved leaders who lead from hurt and fear.*
> —Brené Brown

Brené Brown (2010) rose to worldwide fame following her TED Talk "The Power of Vulnerability." Her lecture and subsequent books inherently changed who I am as a human and the way I work as a leader. She constantly amazes me with her incredible quotes (such as the preceding one) and the way she combines research and her own life experience to explain her point, all of which is based on years of research into vulnerability and shame.

In her work, Brown discusses the power of courage, authenticity, love, and connection, and specifically the power of losing the behaviors that you think you should demonstrate and being authentically who you are. In her research, people who let go of these assumed behaviors readily acknowledged the key role that vulnerability played in their lives, particularly when taking risks when there were no guarantees. Brown's work proves, as she constantly preaches, that vulnerability is not weakness. In fact, vulnerability is fundamental to success.

> *I think a lot of people are reluctant to express vulnerability because they persist with a model of leadership that's based on being the expert. And I think the days of that serving us are long gone. Our work is too complex. But vulnerability isn't showing weakness—I think the most powerful way of demonstrating vulnerability is asking for help in an authentic way.*
> —Catherine Jackson, former school and system leader

Brené Brown states that vulnerability is the birthplace of joy, love, creativity, and belonging. Brown talks about the importance of practicing gratitude daily and leaning in with love and joy—especially in challenging situations. Although her initial work into shame and vulnerability did not explicitly focus on leadership, her more recent work in this area emphasizes the power of vulnerability for leaders. In *Daring Greatly*, Brown (2015a) calls on leaders to accept the challenge of leading from the heart and showing vulnerability, rather than leading from a place of fear and distrust. She states:

> *What we know matters. But who we are matters more. Being, rather than knowing, requires showing up and letting ourselves be seen. It requires us to dare greatly, to be vulnerable. The first step of that journey is understanding where we are, what we're up against, and where we need to go. (p. 16)*

As a leader who is guiding a data-informed team through the process of change, showing vulnerability is key.

In step 3 (page 77), I highlighted the importance of being courageously transparent and openly discussing targets, data, and tracking results with staff and students.

This idea can raise concerns for some leaders because of the vulnerability it requires. Sharing your goals and aspirations and showing your authentic self can be daunting. A common reaction to this idea is, "What if I show them who I am, and they don't like it?" because it is easier to fail or to not be accepted when we do not show our true selves. Leaders might ask questions such as, What if I name a goal to staff and we don't get there? What if we do not achieve what we set out to do? How is this going to reflect on me and my leadership? Am I going to lose respect as the leader of this team? But if you continue as you are, wearing your mask and not taking risks, what if you end up not catering for student needs as best you can? Better yet, what if you do set aspirational goals and reach them? How will that reflect on you and your team?

AN EXAMPLE OF VULNERABILITY AND SCHOOL LEADERSHIP

As a consultant, I have worked with a variety of leaders inhabiting a range of positions on the continuum of "happily embracing vulnerability" to "guarded self-protection." One leader, who showed little vulnerability and was determined to not have anyone think he cared too much about the data and school results, struggled to lead change in his school because staff did not feel empowered by him. They never saw a personable or relatable side to this principal, and because they didn't feel as though he valued them, the staff felt as though he didn't trust them to do their jobs well. Over time, the distance that the leader created between himself and his team developed into a culture of fear and accountability. His teachers did what they did not because they saw the value in it or bought into school improvement efforts but because they feared the consequences of them not following the plan. They were motivated by the fear of being reprimanded or losing their job rather than by understanding and buying into the vision of the school.

On the other hand, I worked with a principal who actively sought to develop the vulnerability he showed in his leadership. It did not come naturally or automatically, but he prioritized this as a growth area and took the opportunity to show his staff that he was just like them. Staff knew why he loved teaching, saw him in their classrooms and spending time with students, and understood his values. He shared stories of his life; staff had even met his family. Because of all this, they genuinely believed what he was doing was the right thing for the students, even if they didn't necessarily agree with all his decisions. This principal's storytelling and sharing of his experiences connected with other staff emotionally, and they could draw parallels between themselves and him, which is something that storytelling has been proven to do (Jackson & Jackson, 2018; Tableau Software, 2019).

By valuing authenticity and vulnerability, and showing that he didn't always have all the answers and that he wanted to hear and learn from others, this principal had incredible buy-in from staff. When asked, staff could easily and confidently articulate the school vision and goals and detail the steps they were taking collectively to achieve them. It was a vastly different culture from that of the first example, as staff actively worked alongside the principal and saw themselves as members of a team that was creating real change. They adopted shared responsibility for the improvement and knew the role that they played in the change process.

THE VULNERABILITY CONTINUUM

I almost always conduct my work with leaders who are somewhere in between these two examples. Most principals are aware that a shift in demonstrable leadership characteristics is necessary and know that a fear-based approach will not build the long-term motivation or results they are looking for from their staff. The old, power-driven leadership paradigm is most familiar to them, and they know that they need a new approach, but they cannot completely hand over control and often drift back into their default practice.

Many leaders struggle to move from their previous approaches to a position that is more vulnerable and leans in with love. This will never be a quick shift along the continuum, as such a shift requires some people to unlearn all the models and templates of leadership that they have witnessed and worked with throughout their career. But I wholeheartedly believe that all leaders will see improvements in the culture of their school as soon as their approaches and practices begin to shift along the vulnerability continuum.

A good way to begin this challenge is to think about the language that you use when speaking with members of your community. Start by using collaborative language with your teams and ask for their input, such as the following.

- "I've been thinking of new ways to approach this—do you have any ideas on what we could do?"
- "How do you think we could approach this?"
- "I'm a bit stuck on this and can't understand why it is happening—what do you think?"

The use of "we" and "us" indicates to your staff that you see yourselves as a team that is in this together. Your change agenda will not succeed without their input, and so you need to show that you value their contribution. Slowly but surely, by demonstrating some vulnerability and showing that you are willing to learn from others, you will cede some of the traditional management power and cultivate teams that want to work with and for you, and go above and beyond to help you achieve your goals, in return. Even when leaders take a small step back along this continuum, effective leaders keep trying and strive to embrace vulnerability.

LENCIONI'S DYSFUNCTIONS OF A TEAM

Lencioni's (2002) model of five dysfunctions of a team relates to the discussion of vulnerability in the first and most foundational level—the absence of trust.

Lencioni states that teams cannot function effectively without professional trust, as participants question their role in the group, the role of their leaders, and whether the leader believes that they have a purpose or place in the group. He believes that a key strategy for counteracting a lack of trust, or preventing this risk in the first place, is through the introduction of vulnerability. Once the leader begins to lead from a place of authenticity, acknowledges that he or she does not always have the answers, and genuinely values the contributions of others, then vulnerability and professional trust within the team begin to flow. When team members see their leader value and model vulnerability, they adopt similar approaches and then also begin to show vulnerability.

As the vulnerability of the leader and the team play off one another and continue to increase, so does professional trust. As trust builds, team members feel as though their position in the group is valued and important, and the leader is more open and transparent with their teams. This leads to significantly greater buy-in from staff. As Brené Brown states in her book *Daring Greatly* (2015a):

> *The snowball starts rolling when a leader is willing to be vulnerable with his or her subordinates. . . . This act of vulnerability is predictably perceived as courageous by team members and inspires others to follow suit. (p. 54)*

Similarly, Frances Frei (2018), speaking about building professional trust in an organization, challenges leaders to embrace authenticity and encourage it in staff members:

> *To the leaders in the room, it is your obligation to set the conditions that not only make it safe for us to be authentic but make it welcome, make it celebrated, cherish it for exactly what it is, which is the key for us achieving greater excellence than we have ever known is possible.*

KEY SUMMARY

- Step 5 requires you and your team to sit with the data, analyze the information in front of you, and identify the evident trends.

- Showing vulnerability will support this process by encouraging a culture of authenticity and trust rather than one of inaccuracy, misrepresentation, or distrust.

- The leadership paradigm has shifted. Leaders with "power" are out; leaders who show authenticity and vulnerability are in.

- Authenticity and vulnerability will assist you in the ways in which you have data-informed conversations with members of your team.

- Lead with authenticity, and you will model this behavior to others in your team. They will see that vulnerability is valued and will follow your lead. They too will embrace vulnerability, and the efforts will snowball into a much more authentic workplace.

- Lack of authenticity leads to a culture of limited or no professional trust.

- If you want to build professional trust, show vulnerability and lead with authenticity.

REFLECTION QUESTIONS

During the process of analyzing the trends in the data, use the following questions to reflect on the progress you and your team are making.

- Do you demonstrate vulnerability with your colleagues? If not, why not? What more could you do to move along the vulnerability continuum?

- Do you ask others for help? Why or why not?

- Are you brave enough to tell others that you don't have all the answers? Why or why not? What concerns do you have about this?

- If someone else was asked about your willingness to encourage others to voice their opinions, contribute to conversations about student data, and offer alternate viewpoints to your own, how would he or she describe you? Would you be happy with that description?

- Would your staff say that you are actively involved and truly present in professional learning, in meetings, and when working with staff and students?

- Of the list of questions to support your analysis, which do you find

  - Most interesting?

  - Most challenging?

  - Most useful?

- Which questions will you choose to use at this stage of your analysis?

- How do you show people implicitly and explicitly that you value the contributions that they make toward achieving team goals? How can you do this better?

- Do your staff feel trusted by you? How do you actively build that feeling of trust?

- Is this project truly your priority? If so, what are the logistical changes that you need to make to your schedule to ensure you are actively engaged and present every time you need to be?

chapter eight

QUESTION THE REASONS FOR TRENDS

Step 6 requires you to both demonstrate and encourage curiosity in questioning and exploring reasons for trends in the data. In the previous step (see chapter 7, page 97), you identified the trends and prioritized their importance or relevance but did not consider possible reasons for them. While you might be able to quickly and easily identify one or two possible reasons for a particular trend, you need to sit with the data and spend time considering alternate reasons for trends to anticipate all potential causes. Having your team working around and with you ensures that you consider multiple perspectives, which is vital at the stage where storytelling begins.

Start this task by writing each separate trend identified in figure 7.8 (page 107) in the middle of a large piece of paper—one trend per piece of paper. Put these papers up on the walls around the room and split your team into smaller groups so that two to three staff members are standing at each poster. Give your team time to brainstorm and list all the possible reasons why the trend might have occurred. After five minutes, have team members rotate to the next station, spending the same amount of time at each poster reading the other members' reasons and then detailing their own thoughts on why a particular trend might have occurred. Continue moving through the stations until each team member has had the opportunity to contribute to every trend discussion. Following the final station, have the last group that contributed to each poster read out all the possible reasons for the particular trend. You can extend this discussion if needed, but ensure that you record any other observations or comments on the appropriate poster. The brainstorm pages might look like the ones in figure 8.1.

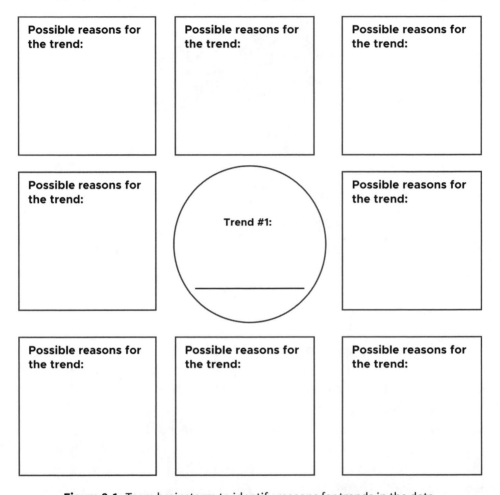

Figure 8.1: Team brainstorm to identify reasons for trends in the data.

Depending on the number of trends that you identified in step 5, you will need to be discerning about the number of brainstorming templates that you complete. You may see the value in considering all the trends that you listed, or you might identify that some of the possible reasons appear across data trends. If it makes more sense to collapse some of the trends into broader areas or select only the top three trends to investigate in this step, then do so. Do not waste the team's time doing an analysis of ten different data trends if you do not intend to follow through with those issues at the next step. Only choose to explore the trends that will have the greatest impact if you are able to make changes.

PRIMING THE ENVIRONMENT BY ENCOURAGING CURIOSITY

> *Being curious means being open to new information and actively seeking it out. It means embracing facts that don't fit your worldview and trying to understand their implications. It means letting your mistakes trigger curiosity instead of embarrassment. . . . It is quite exciting being curious, because it means you are always discovering something interesting.*
> —Dr. Hans Rosling

At a 2019 conference in Sydney, Jen Jackson—co-founder of employee experience company Jaxzyn— spoke about the meaning of curiosity. She stated that etymologically, one of the roots of the word *curious* means "to care." Jackson said that curiosity fuels empathy; it allows us to build connections and is a precursor to learning (Tableau Software, 2019). As educator George Loewenstein (1994) reports, curiosity is piqued when there is a gap between what we know and what we want to know—this gap encourages us to ask questions.

Jackson and Jackson (2018) say, "Curiosity draws our attention and primes us to learn. It has the power to shift mindsets. It can even change the relationships we have with others" (p. 1). The authors state that "the curiosity gap does more than attract our attention; it compels us to learn" (p. 5). While curiosity has much to offer organizations, the adverse effect is that leaders can completely annihilate curiosity by having unrealistic expectations of their teams, providing an inadequate amount of time to resolve the curiosity (both too much and too little time affect curiosity), and developing a culture defined by a fear of failure. Jackson and Jackson (2018) state, "Punishing failure is a great way to crush future curiosity—and potential brilliance along with it" (p. 11). So, by encouraging risk taking, supporting staff when a particular path or plan does not work as they would have liked, and having realistic, yet professionally challenging, aspirations for the team, leaders can build a sense of curiosity and tap into the empathy and learning that it can develop.

While we know that teamwork, open communication, and collaboration are important in teams, so too is curiosity. Your team might be great communicators who function and work well together, but curiosity and the ability to explore alternatives and consider other viewpoints and possibilities are key to leading an effective organizational team. Curiosity is also particularly important when attempting to use data analysis and visualizations to build the data storytelling.

THE ROLE OF CURIOSITY IN DATA-INFORMED CHANGE

When leading data-informed teams through the change process, curiosity is important in how we explore options for trends identified in the data and the ways in which we respond to them. Leaders should always embrace and celebrate curiosity (and the conversations that come about through having a curious team), because without it we may always respond in the same way to the same problem, even though there could be better ways of addressing it. There is never one single reason for a particular trend or result, as nothing ever happens in a simple cause-and-effect relationship in schools. Therefore, by being curious, the leader and his or her team can identify possible options for trends in the data and then explore these further. Change can then take place once the team has considered all the options.

One benefit of having a team specifically focused on a single project in your school is that it enables more of your staff to be involved in this process—and the more brains, the better. By having a team of people around you who take time to consider the reasons, brainstorm solutions, and use their own perspectives to think and view the data curiously, the more likely you are to identify the correct trends and implement more appropriate strategies for improvement. The storytelling is guaranteed to improve when there are more people contributing to the conversation!

DATA WISE PROJECT

In the second chapter of this book (page 25), I discussed the Data Wise Project run by Harvard University's Graduate School of Education. Other than teaching educators the required steps to progress through data-informed change, the facilitators of the program realized they also needed to address the attributes or characteristics of the person and team approaching the data. In a way, it is their own version of priming the environment, but they only discuss three key attributes, which they call the *ACE Habits of Mind*. In this model, "A stands for a shared commitment to Action, Assessment, and Adjustment; C stands for Intentional Collaboration; and E stands for a relentless focus on Evidence" (Boudett & City, 2013).

Boudett and City (2013) state that following the steps by themselves will not lead to change, but instead, that teachers and leaders need the three habits of mind to ensure the process is effective. While these factors tie in with some of the twelve key elements for priming the environment that I discuss throughout this book, I mention the habits of mind at this point for their focus on intentional collaboration and a willingness to adjust. Similar to the discussion on curiosity and developing a team that comes together to analyze the data, the Data Wise Project considers that teams meeting and being willing to adjust to alternative viewpoints and options are two key habits of mind required for effective data-informed change.

If the notion of curiosity is daunting, and you are worried that it may show people that you don't have all the answers, consider the adverse. What happens if you make a quick decision by yourself without exploring all the factors, or if you miss a key reason why the data and the trends are the way they are? If you do not accurately identify the correct reason for a trend, you will invest time and effort in the wrong areas.

For example, if you believe that the standardized testing results dropped because your writing program is not working, but in fact it is one teacher's class data that are skewing the results, you run the risk of removing an effective program and missing the fact that a teacher is negatively affecting student results. And what happens the next year? With the writing program gone, students have fewer effective activities to practice their writing, and the teacher that neither agrees with standardized testing nor encourages his or her students to try their hardest will still be doing the same thing. Your results will continue to decline until you realize the real reason for the drop and make changes. While all of this is happening, your team of teaching staff will be looking for guidance, unsure of whether your ideas are having an impact and questioning your logic in removing the writing program, until they learn that you missed the mark when the results do not change.

Encouraging others to be inquisitive with and alongside you builds the authenticity and trustworthiness of your leadership. By understanding your logic, and seeing that you learn from others and value their contributions, your team will be more receptive to you and your approaches and more likely to trust and want to support you. Remember, knowledge is no longer power—your teams expect you to ask questions and learn with them, not dictate what they have to do and how they have to approach challenges.

THINKING FAST AND SLOW

In his book *Thinking, Fast and Slow*, Daniel Kahneman (2011) outlines two systems of thinking: system 1 and system 2. The notion of taking time and exploring and thinking deeply about solutions is a good example of system 2 thinking.

In a generalized sense, system 1 thinking is fast, automatic, and more emotional decision making. It is what Kahneman refers to as *thinking fast*. On the other hand, system 2 thinking is measured, calculated, more logical, and more complex. It is referred to as *thinking slow*. Throughout his book, Kahneman discusses the prevalence of system 1 thinking in our worlds—it is the dominant thinking system even though it sometimes runs into problems, and it is used a lot more than we think. System 1 thinking leads us to jump to conclusions that are not well thought out or that are overconfident while not considering all the evidence.

When using, analyzing, and responding to educational data in schools, system 1 thinking is evident in dismissive comments about students such as, "Oh well, we know what he is like," "She must have had a bad day," or "He is just not good at writing." Other than not showing students much respect, these responses are superficial, are dominated by fear and blame, and do not lead to any real change or solutions. System 1 responses in our context are often narrow views of students and their abilities that have not required much thought—many of which may tap into negativity bias. Teachers and leaders who make comments such as these have not thought logically, rationally, or at any length about the data and have not considered a range of potential solutions to the problem. Similarly, a system 1 response to high-performance data or good results would reach a conclusion about why a student or cohort achieved particularly good results without investigating the full range of reasons. Without thorough investigation or consideration, system 1 thinking in this instance could potentially lead to incorrect assumptions about the results.

Conversely, system 2 thinking in a data-informed educational context would ask measured questions about the disappointing data and results, consider different viewpoints, discuss opinions, look for alternative answers, consider the range of factors that affected the results, and not be hijacked by blame, shame, or a teacher's personal views of a student or cohort. System 2 thinking might seek advice from others to learn more about the student or cohort and their results and take time to consider all the possible reasons and options for low results. In a case where a team was looking at results that were positive, system 2 thinkers would consider in a measured and rational manner the reasons why the growth and improvement occurred with a view to replicating those conditions to assist other students.

Sometimes these system 2 conversations tap into teachers' curiosity, and so the exploration and analyses of the results might take considerable time, but this approach is proven to be far more effective and accurate than jumping to quick conclusions. System 2 thinking excels in intense analyses and problem-solving challenges like those found when using and analyzing data drawn from complex and dynamic contexts, such as our schools. True analysis and change can only occur when system 2 thinking is utilized because the real causes and considerations of trends in the data are more likely to come to light, allowing for teams to flesh out and rationally plan practical next steps.

AN EXAMPLE OF CURIOSITY AND
DATA-INFORMED CHANGE

I once worked with a school that had low national testing writing results, which did not align with the school-based writing task implemented every term or their English learning area results. Literacy had been a focus area for the school over a number of years, so their English and school writing task results were improving, but the national testing results had dropped each year over the previous three years. Because I was the external consultant, it was easier for me to approach the data with curiosity as there was no risk that I would be blamed for the low results and staff were not asking me to justify what had gone wrong.

Being in that position meant I was able to ask difficult questions, explore possible reasons for the trends objectively, and more easily use my system 2 thinking than the teachers and leaders who were close to the data. I didn't know the teachers or the students, and so I remained mindful that I had to tread slowly, as I was learning about the data for the first time in this context, whereas the teachers and leaders within the school dealt with them regularly and had a better contextual understanding than I did.

As a result of the curiosity and system 2 thinking that I brought to the exercise, I was able to ask different questions of the leadership team than they had considered previously. Their initial system 1 reaction was that student performance and their writing and reading were all improving, and that the school-based learning area results and writing practice proved that they were making progress. But students were clearly not doing well in the external exams, and so they believed exam stress and anxiety were solely to blame. While these factors may have contributed to a certain extent, I identified four factors that the leadership team had not considered: (1) the teaching team, (2) a schoolwide focus on writing, (3) the impact of particular teacher mindsets on the results, and (4) the accuracy or moderation of in-school measures. It wasn't my curiosity alone that helped me ask different questions of the leadership team; utilizing my system 2 thinking and taking time with my different understanding of the situation helped me build questions and options for their context.

While the leadership team in the school previously had not considered the possible reasons for the decline in data that I asked them about, identifying reasons for trends generally becomes easier when a team of staff objectively considers the data. The reality is that no matter how much experience we have in the education sector or as a leader, we will never have all the answers. We need people in our teams to add their perspective and encourage us to consider other options.

Instead of being fearful of how this will reflect on you as a leader, embrace the opportunity to develop members of your team and have them help you investigate reasons and solutions. Welcome people into your team who challenge your views and offer different perspectives rather than surrounding yourself with people who agree with all your ideas. By bringing more people along with you, you will develop the capacity of your team members, and it is more likely that your interpretation of events will be accurate. Embrace the opportunity to be curious and show your team that you value this characteristic in them. Use collaborative language like "us," "we," and "our students." Establish systems and processes in your school that encourage your teachers to ask the important questions, utilize their system 2 thinking, and find solutions to the challenges that they face. This may require you to be creative in the way that you timetable and schedule opportunities for this analysis to occur, but the rewards outweigh the effort required to establish the systems in the first place.

PRIMING THE ENVIRONMENT BY LEANING INTO DIFFICULT CONVERSATIONS

When leading a team through data-informed change, the ugly truth you have to accept is that there will inevitably be data that do not reflect the time and effort that you and your staff have put in. Some data will be hard to digest—not because the analysis is difficult but because things do not always work out the way we want them to, despite our best efforts. Consequently, there will be times when your self-reflection is difficult to stomach, or when you need to have difficult conversations with the teams or individuals you are leading. When used incorrectly, data have the potential to frighten people and activate a survive, rather than a thrive, response (Kotter, 2017). Your role as a leader is to use data in a way that is supportive and encouraging, and to have those difficult conversations with your staff when you need to. The risk of activating a survive response should never discourage you from having the conversation in the first place.

AN EXAMPLE OF LEANING INTO DIFFICULT CONVERSATIONS

I once did some consultancy work in a school in southeast Queensland, Australia, that had varied results. Their school-based data were quite good. Students had been in a structured reading program for a number of years, school-based writing results were improving, and there were normal distributions in learning area results. But standardized national testing results were significantly lower than their in-school assessments, and so I was asked to identify and explain some reasons for the divergent data.

Upon inspection, I realized that there was a clear trend with one particular class that was underperforming. While those students had performed quite well in the years prior to entering their current teacher's class, in that year their results dropped considerably. Some students went from the top end of standardized testing results to at or below the national minimum standard. The school leadership team was unsurprised when I told them about this trend—apparently the teacher was not always supportive of school change and in some instances tried to (not so subtly) derail their improvement efforts. I was asked to work with the teacher to alert this person to the issues, identify some solutions, and support the teacher in ensuring that the results were not considerably lower in the future.

While I enjoy working with staff in this manner, the senior leaders in the school made it clear that they did not want to be the bad guys in having this difficult conversation. They felt that questioning the teacher or bringing the data to her attention would cause the teacher to respond negatively and make it difficult to work with her in the future. The senior leaders knew that the issue needed to be addressed and that they did not want to see similar results in the following year, but they wanted to maintain their relationship with the teacher and make me have the difficult conversation instead. When I spoke to her, the teacher's reaction was neither negative nor positive—she seemed more worried about how she was being perceived by an external consultant. But during the meeting, she did take the time to consider how she might do things differently in the future to help her students achieve.

While I made some progress with this teacher, I question the value of an external consultant having that conversation as opposed to a member of the leadership team. I didn't know her, had never worked with her, and didn't understand the school context, so I find it difficult to understand why I was seen as the best person to have that discussion. Surely a member of the leadership team would have a better relationship with the teacher than I did, understand her story, and know the students that needed discussing? If a member of that team had initiated the discussion instead, he or she could have checked in with the teacher a month later to see how things were going. I couldn't do that, and yet I was chosen to have that difficult conversation.

When the data show you that a teacher or a team is not doing enough for a group of students, you need to help them see the data and support them in making effective changes that will lead to improvements. Your discomfort in initiating the difficult conversation is nowhere near as important as having the conversation is for the students who are being affected. They are the reason why it is important that you have the conversation in the first place. Always lead with this as your focus. I have since focused on building these skills with leaders so that they feel empowered to have these conversations themselves. I found it unsurprising when talking to the CEO of a leadership firm in Australia who said, "Everyone wants training in two things at the moment—data and difficult conversations" (personal communication, October 15, 2019).

LENCIONI'S DYSFUNCTIONS OF A TEAM

Patrick Lencioni (2002) refers to the importance of having difficult conversations in his five dysfunctions of a team. Having difficult conversations sits at the second-lowest level of the pyramid but is also related to the second-highest level in the pyramid, the avoidance of accountability. Lencioni discusses the power of positive conflict and divergent teams and ideas. He states that teams that constantly agree do not challenge one another and do not reach the heights that they may have otherwise. As the leader, you must encourage team members to have their say, and to participate and question ideas, in order to maximize the impact that your team has.

Similarly, if and when difficult conversations need to occur, you need to be willing to have them. Lencioni states that the earlier the conversation can occur, the better, as it minimizes the length of time and impact of the negative behavior and it could stop the behavior at an earlier point than if it is left longer. Lencioni recommends that leaders should not let personal discomfort get in the way of having these conversations. He also states that leaders need to be consistent in the way that they have these conversations—in what they will tolerate and what they will leave to other members of the team to address.

SCHOOL LEADERS' REFLECTIONS ON DIFFICULT CONVERSATIONS

I had the opportunity to ask some school leaders about their advice for other leaders in having difficult conversations in the workplace. Wayne Chapman, a first-year principal, stated:

> These conversations are challenging and should be handled slightly differently depending upon the context. In all cases leaders must be clear about the issue. Research. Research. Research. Present the issue to be addressed in clear, unemotive terms, and ask questions. Generally, people are operating from a position where they are trying their best to do their best job. Challenging conversations with these people, while difficult, are easier than those with people who do not have the best interests of students at heart. When people appear to be operating out of alignment with the organization and goals of the college, direct honesty is the best approach; call the behavior as you see it. (W. Chapman, personal communication, June 19, 2019)

In a way, Wayne has referred to the easier conversations occurring with employees with a high willingness to do the right thing—that is, people who want to work with and for you in your organization. Staff who do not have that desire can certainly be difficult to have these conversations with!

Catherine Jackson, a former school leader and system leader, stated:

> *Try to do more asking than telling. For example, "I noticed this; how did you think that went?" In my experience, most people know if things don't go well. If you take the time to ask and to listen, you'll find you have to do a lot less telling. People get worried about the telling, so I think asking is a much healthier start, and it keeps you out of blame and judgement for just a little bit longer. Remember, the standard you walk past is the standard you accept. It's by dealing with the little things early on that we avoid ultimately having to deal with huge problems down the track. (C. Jackson, personal communication, June 24, 2019)*

Interestingly, Catherine's approach is focused on learning about what is going on from the perspective of the employee in the conversation with the leader. But like Wayne, Catherine's experience suggests that staff who want to learn and are reflective of their practice can be easier to work with in difficult conversations. Also, Catherine's response taps into Lencioni's advice about acting quickly—have the conversation when the issue is smaller, rather than waiting for it to escalate, when it requires a bigger and more difficult conversation.

Terry O'Connor, a former head of campus and current teacher coach and mentor, gave the following advice on having difficult conversations.

- If there is an area of leadership that is most discussed between leaders, it is the difficult conversation. The reality is that no one approach fits every difficult conversation, but there are a few generic considerations.
- At the heart of the discussion is the core issue that the leader wants to address. This should be clearly articulated at the start to leave no doubt in the mind of the teacher.
- Consider whether there are any underlying issues for the teacher which may be affecting the matter. Given the underlying issues, what can be offered as support for the teacher?

- What short-term and long-term goals can be put in place to progress the issue?
- Are there professional development opportunities that may also support and assist in follow-up discussions? (T. O'Connor, personal communication, June 27, 2019)

As a leader in your organization, you need to accept that there will be difficult conversations that you need to have with staff, and this extends to the realm of using and analyzing school data. The reality is that some teachers are more effective or will get better results than others. Inevitably, we all make mistakes. It is your role to have these conversations and support your staff through the data-informed change process.

BRENÉ BROWN ON DIFFICULT CONVERSATIONS

In Brené Brown's books *Daring Greatly* (2015a) and *Rising Strong* (2015b), she talks about the importance of leaders accepting discomfort and leaning into it rather than pulling away. In *Rising Strong*, Brown (2015b) talks about three key common traits in transformative and resilient leaders:

> *First, they recognize the central role that relationships and story play in culture and strategy, and they stay curious about their own emotions, thoughts, and behaviors. Second, they understand and stay curious about how emotions, thoughts, and behaviors are connected in the people they lead, and how those factors affect relationships and perception. And third, they have the ability and willingness to lean in to discomfort and vulnerability. (p. 8)*

As a leader, Brown emphasizes the importance of leaning into the discomfort and the feeling of vulnerability in the third characteristic because her research indicates that these are important elements of transformative and resilient leaders. But it is also important to note that this was the *third* characteristic. Without a willingness to recognize the other two factors—the central role of relationships and the connectivity of emotions—in the first instance, leaning into discomfort would be incredibly difficult.

But the notion of leaning into discomfort is much broader than just the leadership skills that you demonstrate. In *Daring Greatly*, Brown (2015a) writes that you should also encourage this characteristic in the teams that you work with to nurture a culture of discomfort:

> *The goal is not "getting comfortable with hard conversations" but normalizing discomfort. If leaders expect real learning, critical thinking, and change, then discomfort should be normalized: "We believe growth and learning are uncomfortable so it's going to happen here—you're going to feel that way. We want you to know that it's normal and it's an expectation here. You're not alone and we ask that you stay open and lean into it." (p. 198)*

So, by encouraging discomfort in your teams; showing authenticity and vulnerability in your leadership; knowing the ways that thoughts, behaviors, and emotions impact the team dynamic; and genuinely wanting to work with and develop your team, you are building a culture where difficult conversations become just that little bit easier.

JIM KNIGHT ON BETTER CONVERSATIONS

Educational researcher Jim Knight has gained worldwide recognition for his work on difficult conversations. In his book *Better Conversations: Coaching Ourselves and Each Other to Be More Credible, Caring, and Connected*, Knight (2016) advocates for "better conversations." He believes that too many conversations in schools become top-down conversations when only a few of them need to be. The rest, he says, should be better.

Knight's book takes readers through six beliefs and ten habits about better conversations. The six beliefs of having better conversations are as follows.

1. I see conversation partners as equals.
2. I want to hear what others have to say.
3. I believe people should have a lot of autonomy.
4. I don't judge others.
5. Conversation should be back and forth.
6. Conversation should be life-giving.

He suggests that if we were to approach our conversations with these beliefs in mind (and the other party did as well), the outcomes and productivity from the conversation would have much greater impact than a top-down approach. To think that consultants need to work with people in developing these theoretically simplistic ideas is, in many respects, a sad and concerning fact of the system and the times in which we work.

Further, Knight suggests ten habits for people to have better conversations. These habits will take time to develop, and some people will have different strengths in different aspects, but all of them are worth practicing and implementing in your conversations. These habits are as follows.

1. Demonstrating empathy
2. Listening with empathy
3. Fostering dialogue
4. Asking better questions
5. Making emotional connections
6. Being a witness to the good
7. Finding common ground
8. Controlling toxic emotions
9. Redirecting toxic conversations
10. Building trust

While a full discussion of these beliefs and habits is outside the scope of this book, I would strongly encourage you to discover Knight's work if having difficult and better conversations is something you intend to practice in your leadership.

KEY SUMMARY

- In Step 6, you need to sit with your team to question the reasons for the trends in the data.

- Curiosity is a key requirement when it comes to leading data-informed teams through change. Curiosity allows you to consider different alternatives and different solutions, meaning you are more likely to identify an effective path forward.

- Encouraging curiosity encourages learning and leads to open mindsets and approaches. This is far more effective than closed mindsets and no desire to learn!

- Talk with your team about system 1 and system 2 thinking. Encourage them to use their system 2 thinking and different perspectives to consider alternate viewpoints and options for change.

- As a leader, you must demonstrate and model a commitment to curiosity and system 2 thinking if you would like your team to adopt a similar approach. Do so by taking time to consider the possibilities, asking questions, and encouraging others to offer alternate explanations.

- Remember, you are walking the path alongside your team members and learning with them. You will never have all the answers, and that is OK. Show your team that you are committed to learning with them and that you value their contribution by listening and showing vulnerability.

- If there are things that need addressing, you need to have the conversation, even if you do not feel particularly comfortable doing so. As a leader, it is far better for you to have the conversation rather than not have it—or if you rely on an external consultant to do the dirty work!

- Lean into difficult conversations with love. Be compassionate and approach the conversation as a way of supporting the teacher. Ask what he or she thinks of the data. Center the conversation around student learning and remember the importance of relationship and story.

- The standard you walk past is the standard you accept. Hold people accountable and have the conversations earlier rather than later.

REFLECTION QUESTIONS

During the process of analyzing the trends in the data, use the following reflection questions to reflect on the progress you and your team are making.

- What are your views on system 1 and system 2 thinking? Why do you have these views?

- What is an example of a time when you used system 1 thinking and it did not work out well? What was the outcome? What was the impact? What did you learn from the experience?

- Share your example of when system 1 thinking was not effective with your team. Is there anything that makes you uncomfortable about the idea of sharing the story as a learning experience?

- How do you approach difficult conversations? How could you have better conversations with staff in the future?

- Looking specifically at Jim Knight's beliefs on better conversations, do you agree with the six statements that he makes? Why or why not? Which is the biggest challenge for you? How might you overcome this challenge?

- Looking specifically at Jim Knight's ten habits to demonstrate in better conversations, do you agree with the ten suggestions he makes? Why or why not? Which poses the biggest challenge for you? How might you overcome this challenge?

- Do you believe that learning and growth are uncomfortable? Why or why not?

- How do you build an effective and safe culture in your school where teachers also believe that learning and growth are uncomfortable? How and when do you actively encourage discomfort?

chapter nine

CONSIDER OPTIONS FOR DATA-INFORMED CHANGE AND CHOOSE YOUR DIRECTION

Once you have identified the reasons for the particular trends in your data in step 6 (see chapter 8, page 115), you need to explore the ways to address those reasons and make changes to tackle the problem. Again, it is important that you utilize both your system 1 and system 2 thinking at this stage. While the quick, reactive response of system 1 thinking might provide you with solutions that you do enact in the long term, make sure that you also access and use system 2 thinking in brainstorming solutions. By discussing potential changes with a team over a longer period of time, you are more likely to access rational, well-thought-out system 2 options.

CONSIDERING DATA-INFORMED CHANGE OPTIONS

In a school outside of Brisbane, Queensland, that I consulted for, my analysis of results made it clear that writing progress and achievement were plummeting at a remarkable pace. While students had previously proved they were quite capable, over time their writing results dropped significantly. Although the school focused on a program to improve reading comprehension, had a schoolwide writing strategy, and displayed above-average numeracy results, something was not working when it came to writing.

Although my immediate, system 1 response might have been to blame the socio-economic status of the students coming in or the local elementary schools, parents, or social media, it was important to consider all the options and potential actions available. Nothing ever occurs in silos in schools, so any intervention or change may have unanticipated impacts and results. Therefore, in considering the options for data-informed change at step 7, this particular school might:

- Work with and write to all parents in the following year about the importance of good literacy skills for life and ask for their support in positively framing writing tasks at school

- Speak with students about their challenges with writing, destigmatize writing, and tell them that teachers are setting some school goals to help them improve and encourage students to try their best

- Speak with staff to ascertain what professional development is required for them to become better teachers of writing, and prioritize their attendance at these sessions

- Award effort prizes for students who try their hardest to improve their writing as well as prizes for students who make the biggest improvements to their writing

- Share success stories with the broader community

- Combine classes where necessary so that stronger literacy teachers coteach and model good practice to other teachers in the same year level

- Ensure all students receive the same message about trying their best, and use middle and senior leaders to support the process

- Talk to the teachers about the trends in the data and ways in which they encourage students to improve their writing; seek their perspectives on why the students are underperforming

- Engage teachers in a data analysis or tracking team to monitor the improvements across the school

The preceding points offer just some examples of the ways in which the school could address the declining results.

Using your team to brainstorm ideas for data-informed change is beneficial, as different members can provide solutions to the problem that you may not have previously considered. At the conclusion of step 7, you should have identified a range of possible changes designed to address each reason for negative trends in the data. As you identify potential solutions, build on your work from step 6 (page 115) and annotate the reasons for the trends with possible changes or adjustments in a figure such as figure 9.1.

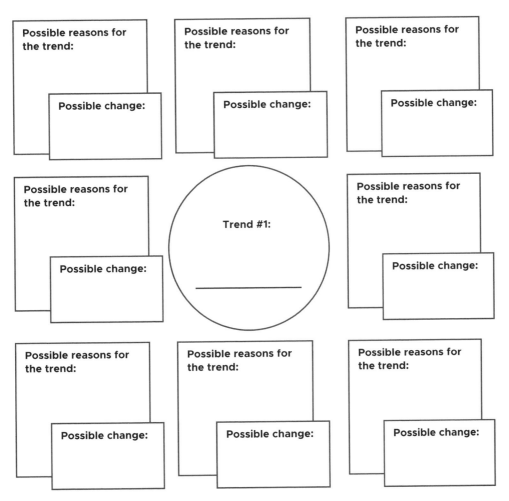

Figure 9.1: Team brainstorm to identify possible change options for negative trends in the data.

PRIMING THE ENVIRONMENT BY BUILDING PROFESSIONAL TRUST

> *It's a chicken or the egg issue. We need to feel trust to be vulnerable. And we need to be vulnerable in order to trust. . . . Trust is a product of vulnerability that grows over time and requires work, attention, and full engagement. Trust isn't a grand gesture.*
> —Brené Brown

A number of the elements for priming the environment for data-informed change require trust, which is vital when building vulnerability and authenticity. But trust is far more multifaceted than just these simple connections.

Brené Brown talks a lot about trust in both our personal lives and the workplace, saying that it is incredibly difficult to define as a concept. In a Super Soul session entitled "The Anatomy of Trust," Brown (2019) refers to a definition of *trust* from Charles Feltman, which says *trust* is "choosing to make something important to you vulnerable to the actions of someone else." Put simply, it is handing over something of importance, not knowing how the other person will act or react. If you trust someone, you feel safe doing this. Conversely, distrust is when you cannot do this or when you feel unsafe sharing something with the recipient.

Brown regularly compares the idea of trust to putting marbles in a jar. Trust is built slowly by little acts of service and kindness over time. It is not the big things that we do but rather the small things, which require regular effort, attention, and presence with members of a team, that add marbles to the jar. At work, trust is built through words and actions, through encouraging team members to take the lead on projects, through communicating openly, by handing over responsibility to others, and by celebrating success. Trust is destroyed by placing blame on individuals or teams, developing smaller groups with their own agenda within the larger group, or by speaking negatively about team members. If any of these things happen, marbles are taken out of the jar—and not necessarily at the same rate they were put in.

Brown talks about the frequency of what she calls *sliding door* moments, in reference to the 1998 Gwyneth Paltrow film where two outcomes depend on whether or not the main character misses her train. While Brown says that trust is built in small acts, the sliding door moments are those times in our day where we choose to either build trust or betray it. Where trust is a culmination of many small instances, Brown says that betrayal is the same—small instances where we choose to ignore or not connect and erode any trust built over time. But if we choose to engage, marbles are put in the jar and trust builds.

Rather than relying on a broad definition, Brené Brown operationalizes trust through seven key elements, from which she developed the acronym BRAVING.

- **Boundaries** refers to having clear boundaries of our own, respecting the boundaries of others, and sticking to them no matter what.
- **Reliability** is built when we do what we say we will do, over and over again. Saying we will do something and only acting on it once is not a sign of reliability.

- **Accountability** is shown when we make a mistake, own it, apologize, and make amends.
- **Vault** represents when what we share with others is held in confidence.
- **Integrity** is when we act from a place of integrity and encourage others to do the same.
- **Nonjudgment** is to not be judged when we ask for help.
- **Generosity** is where the person assumes generously, particularly in times of distress.

As Brown (2019) talks through these in her Super Soul session on the anatomy of trust, she highlights that trust is a two-way street—we need to see these things in others as well as demonstrate them ourselves in order to build trust.

While I completely agree with all of these elements of trust, and I can think of times where all of these have applied to me both personally and professionally, I also like another definition of *integrity* that she offers during this discussion: "integrity is choosing courage over comfort; choosing what's right over what's fun, fast or easy; and practicing your values, not just professing your values" (Brown, 2019). How true that is!

FRANCES FREI ON TRUST

In her TED Talk on building and rebuilding trust, Frances Frei discusses three main elements that have a key impact on the feeling of trust in a professional team: (1) authenticity, (2) rigor in logic, and (3) empathy. Frei (2018) says:

> There's three things about trust. If you sense that I am being authentic, you are much more likely to trust me. If you sense that I have real rigor in my logic, you are far more likely to trust me. And if you believe that my empathy is directed towards you, you are far more likely to trust me. When all three of these things are working, we have great trust. But if any one of these three gets shaky, if any one of these three wobbles, trust is threatened.

At this point, we know authenticity is an obvious inclusion in this list of factors that affect one's trust in another person, but rigor in logic and empathy are interesting additions. Frei indicates that sharing the reasons for your logic with your team is key, and that it needs to be both sound in the first place and communicated well to the team. Without doing so, you run the risk of causing team members to lose trust in the ability and vision of the leader.

Although it is difficult to offer advice on how to improve the quality of your logic, Frei states that the most common logic wobble comes from leaders who are unable to communicate their logic to the team. She suggests taking the listener on a journey (similar to the data storytelling I discussed earlier). To prevent this logic wobble, Frei (2018) says:

> *I implore you, start with your point in a crisp half-sentence, and then give your supporting evidence. This means that people will be able to get access to our awesome ideas, and just as importantly, if you get cut off before you're done . . . you still get credit for the idea, as opposed to someone else coming in and snatching it from you.*

I have no doubt that all of us can think of times in which we haven't understood or seen the logic in decisions in our schools—and personally, I know this contributes to how much trust I have in the team or the individual leader. If I can see the logic in a decision, then I support the idea or process wholeheartedly. But if I do not understand the logic and it is not communicated to me effectively, I know that I begin to question my trust in the leader.

Of the three elements, the most common wobble in teams that leads to an issue with trust is empathy. On this, Frei (2018) states that often, "people just don't believe that we're mostly in it for them, and they believe that we're too self-distracted." Empathy requires time, and if we are constantly busy and do not carve out that time for others, staff notice it. This is incredibly difficult to do well because leaders are always busy juggling competing priorities, but "without revealing empathy, it makes everything harder. Without the benefit of the doubt of trust, it makes everything harder, and then we have less and less time for empathy, and so it goes" (Frei, 2018).

To address this potential wobble, Frei suggests considering what our distractions are and how they affect the empathy that we show others. Once we identify these distractions, then "we can come up with a trigger that gets us to look up, look at the people right in front of us, listen to them, deeply immerse ourselves in their perspectives, then we have a chance of having a sturdy leg of empathy" (Frei, 2018). This is powerful guidance—I particularly like the phrase "deeply immerse ourselves in their perspectives." I think we all know how good it feels when someone is wholly present and immersed in an interaction with you. We should resolve to be leaders who model that level of presence and engagement with all our staff.

> *If you look at the sorts of behaviors that people like Stephen Covey tell us build trust, and then if you look at the sorts of behaviors that people like Brené Brown tell us build vulnerability, there's actually a lot of overlap between those things. And again, I'd highlight asking for help is one of those, listening to people would be on both lists, admitting mistakes, or being prepared just to admit that you just don't know. So those sorts of things both are demonstrations of vulnerability and we know from the literature that they are very powerful in terms of building trust.*
> —Catherine Jackson, former principal and system leader

In the same way that Frei discusses the power of showing empathy, Simon Sinek puts it even more simply. He learned from his friend and mentor Lieutenant General George Flynn that good leaders ask a member of their team how they are and genuinely care about the answer (Koji, 2016). So simple, and yet so difficult at times—but a wonderful example of how to deeply immerse ourselves in another person's perspective.

As a team member in a data-informed context, I have been in situations where I was inherently trusted in my role—and I flourished! I was innovative, engaged, passionate, and enthusiastic (in fact, after running a professional development session at a previous school, the deputy principal told me that I should "rein in my passion for data"). Despite his advice, I created real change and had a positive impact in that role. At other times, I have been in roles where the leaders constantly questioned the decisions I made, second-guessed my actions, and made me feel like I constantly had to justify my approaches, rather than being encouraged to show initiative and lead projects.

While I achieved good outcomes in both scenarios, I did not enjoy my role when there was little professional trust. In fact, I hated it. I felt that my senior leaders did not trust me or my professional judgment, and I even began to question why I was employed in the role in the first place if they didn't think I could do it. On the other hand, when I felt as though I was trusted implicitly and I was encouraged to lead change, I was happier, I enjoyed the work more, and I achieved better results. It is up to us as leaders to make a conscious decision to develop a work climate that encourages team members to flourish, and not limit their capacity.

> *Trust is foundational to everything. A lack of trust is going to impact relationships, it's going to impact collaboration, therefore it's going to impact collective effort and collective efficacy. And the result is going to be that the gifts and talents of the various members of the community are not going to be effectively accessed in the service of the students and the young people that we serve. So, in short, you're not going to get the best out of people if there's no trust, and we need to be getting the best out of every person in the school community.*
> —Catherine Jackson, former principal and system leader

LENCIONI'S DYSFUNCTIONS OF A TEAM

Patrick Lencioni (2002) identifies the absence of trust as the most fundamental of the five flaws of a dysfunctional team. The absence of trust sits, quite conspicuously, as the broad base of the dysfunctional team pyramid. A key area of focus in Lencioni's discussion is the significant role that vulnerability plays in establishing and maintaining trust. When people feel they are seeing authentic and vulnerable leadership that recognizes challenges and limitations, leaders build trust. As leaders build trust, trust within the team builds and members become more willing to show their own vulnerability. Without this, trust is lost.

> *Professional trust is the ultimate currency for school leaders.*
> —Wayne Chapman, principal

ALIGNMENT WITH KOTTER'S CHANGE PROCESS

The notion of trust, although not directly referenced in his work, is a key requirement of Kotter's eight-step change process (see figure 2.1, page 33), particularly in step 5—enable action by removing barriers.

At this stage, the leader seeks to remove barriers and obstacles that do not align with the vision for change as he or she works to implement and initiate new processes and procedures. Trust is key at this stage of the process. Without feeling as though they are trusted, your guiding coalition or change team will not enact the vision effectively and the change process will fall down.

> *At the core of any professional relationship is trust, not friendliness, between individuals. If trust is present, it is the gateway to building the relationship that allows the circle of delegation to grow. However, trust does not mean the leader abdicates responsibility and does not monitor and/or challenge the leaders under his or her responsibility.*
> —Terry O'Connor, former head of campus

If members of your guiding coalition feel trusted, invested in the project, and that their contribution is valued, trusted, and relied on, they will do incredible work for you. They will be proactive and responsive in addressing organizational resistance and work with staff to bring them along on the change process, minimizing and potentially removing barriers for you. But if members of your guiding coalition do not feel trusted by their peers and leaders, it will be difficult for them to authentically and effectively deal with any organizational resistance. It will be almost impossible for them to convince others that the change process is worthwhile and will lead to improvements if they aren't sure of their involvement or place in the process themselves.

DECIDE ON THE DATA-INFORMED CHANGE

At this stage in the process, you will probably have a wide range of changes that could be made. Now your team needs to reflect on all the reasons and changes as a group and prioritize or rank the actions that you believe will have the greatest impact. This is a difficult task. Hypothetically, if you identified six trends, proposed five possible reasons for each trend, and offered two possible changes for each reason, then you would have sixty possible interventions or changes that could be implemented in your school. No matter how efficient your team is, sixty changes would be unmanageable and completely unfair on your staff!

Start this prioritizing and ranking process by considering each trend separately and highlighting or selecting two to three options on each page that the team believes could have the greatest impact. The factors and questions that you should keep in mind when considering which changes to implement (and highlight at this stage) are as follows.

- What will have the greatest impact on student growth and achievement?
- What additional resources are required to make the proposed changes?
- What can realistically be funded and resourced?

- Is there the skill, will, or capacity on staff to lead the change?
- Are there any change options that would be relatively quick or painless, and could lead to quick wins with staff and good outcomes for students?
- What is the core aim of this analysis, and which trends align with the school or project focus or direction?

Once you have considered these factors and decided on the best options for possible change, highlight the selected change options on each page so that each trend template looks like the one in figure 9.2.

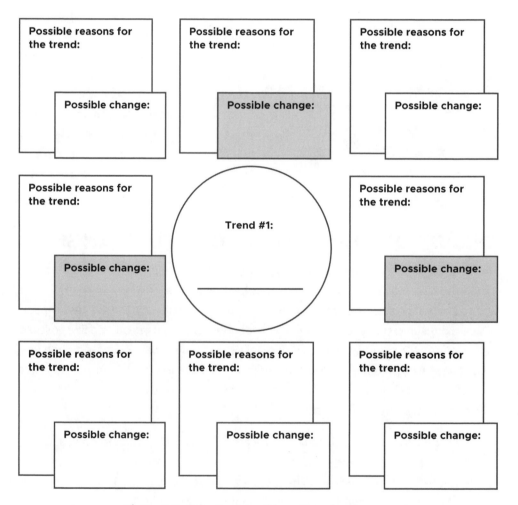

Figure 9.2: Selecting possible options for change.

Enter the two to three possibilities that you have prioritized for each trend into one document or figure. Describe the trend that you noticed in the data from step 5, the possible reasons for the trend from step 6, and the possible changes from step 7. The figure might look like the example in figure 9.3.

Trend description	Possible reasons for the trend	Possible change options	Make the change? Yes/No
Decreased writing results for grade 9 students	1. Teacher skill and understanding of teaching writing	1. Look for professional development opportunities in teaching writing.	
Decreased writing results for grade 9 students	2. One teacher had particularly low results compared to other classes.	2. Create an opportunity for the teacher to coteach with the literacy leader. Re-evaluate after this session.	
Decreased writing results for grade 9 students	3. Teachers don't know how low their student results are and how high they used to be.	3. Allocate time at the next staff meeting to review writing data and plan for writing opportunities.	

Figure 9.3: Example completed template of possible options for change.

Once all the trends, reasons, and possible changes have been entered into the one figure, complete the fourth column as a group. Discuss each of the proposed changes to ascertain the most effective ones for your setting. Choose no more than four strategies to implement from your entire analysis.

Involving all the team members in prioritizing the possible changes benefits the change process as different people will offer unique perspectives and challenges as to why one strategy might work more effectively than another. Generating the list of options in this format also provides you with a list of other changes that could be made in the near future if the process happens quickly and further changes can be made.

While I recommend no more than four changes at this point in the process, this is not a hard-and-fast rule. For example, some of your change solutions may be altering a teacher's timetable, moving a student into another class, or having an external presenter visit the school to lead a professional development session. These are easy and quick wins that will not take much time or effort from members of your teaching staff. In this case, these three actions could be quick to address and enable you to move on to the next change idea that you have.

If you arrive at three suggestions such as introducing a schoolwide writing strategy using a particular resource or structure, implementing short cycles of planning so that teachers meet and plan together every three weeks, and facilitating a writing collection task every term, you are possibly asking too much of your staff in too short a period. In this example, you should start with only one or two of the options or implement one as a whole-school approach and have the other trialed in a small number of classrooms. As the change process gains momentum, you could then have teachers that have been trialing the other initiative share their experience with other teachers and lead the next change cycle.

There is no right or wrong answer to how many changes you can implement immediately. Use your emotional intelligence and your understanding of your staff and context to determine the right number of changes—not so many that they overwhelm teachers but not so few that change is slow and insignificant.

KEY SUMMARY

- Step 7 requires you to consider the options that you have to act on the trends in the data. Explore a range of options for action and list them on the same template as the identified trends. Then, prioritize and decide on the possible options for change, and make decisions about which changes you will implement.

- A culture of professional trust leads to a staff being engaged, enthusiastic, and motivated. Without trust, staff may be apathetic and disengaged.

- Value the role that trust plays in the success of your team.

- Demonstrate empathy, show the rigor in your logic, and be authentic in order to build and rebuild trust. Ask people how they are, and actually care about the answer!

- If required, discuss as a group the importance of professional trust and what professional trust looks like. Set parameters for the way you will work as a team.

- Actions speak far louder than words. Don't just tell your team that you trust them; show that you trust your team by handing over responsibility of tasks, involving them in decision making, and having them convey key messages to the broader teaching team.

- Choose two or three options for change for each trend or issue that you have identified, and then summarize the trend, reasons, and options into the format shown in figure 9.3 (page 141).

- Consider questions relating to resourcing, staff capacity, quick wins, and what is practical in your context to decide which are the best change options for the trends that you have identified.

- From this list, prioritize no more than four options for change. If there are other options in the table that you intend to work through at a later date, record the time that you will begin to focus on the change.

REFLECTION QUESTIONS

During the process of exploring options for potential change in your school and selecting which changes to implement, use the following questions to reflect on the progress you and your team are making.

- What are the ways that you actively build trust in your teams? Do you do any of the following?
    - Demonstrate trust through words and actions.
    - Lead with authenticity and vulnerability.
    - Encourage others to take the lead and hand over responsibility to others.
    - Encourage open communication.
    - Celebrate success.
    - Do what you say you will do and follow through with your actions.
    - Share information in confidence with others and respect others' privacy when they share information in confidence with you.
    - Take ownership of your mistakes and apologize genuinely when you hurt others.
    - Show empathy by looking at the person in front of you, listening to him or her, and deeply immersing yourself in his or her perspective.
    - Prevent logic wobbles by explaining the rigor in your logic to others.

- In the preceding list, what are your areas of strength? What do you need to work on?
- What are the ways that you might erode trust in your teams? Do you do any of the following?
  - Blame individuals or teams for things that don't go to plan.
  - Encourage or ignore small groups that develop with their own agendas.
  - Speak negatively about members of your team or staff when they are not in the room.
- If you were to score your integrity on a scale of one to five, with five being the highest score, how would you score yourself?
- Why did you give yourself that score? Do you do any of the following?
  - Choose courage over comfort.
  - Choose what is right over what is fun or easy.
  - Practice your values, not just profess them.
- How do you build these traits in members of your team?
- What is the right amount of change for your teachers and school community?
- What are the factors that affect their readiness, capacity, and willingness to be involved in the change process?
- Possible questions to think about when choosing the processes to implement are as follows.
  - What resources will you need to lead change in the areas that you have identified?
  - What funding will you need to allocate?
  - How will you cover staff for training or upskilling?
  - What is the impact on the timetable?

chapter ten

CREATE AN ACTION PLAN

In step 7 (page 131), you decided on the changes that you will make, and now you need to think about how each of these will occur. Some changes will be easier than others (for example, moving a teacher from teaching a particular grade level in the following year versus restructuring your school timetable), but it is important to think through the steps, the communication required, the staff involved, and the impact on stakeholders.

CHANGE TO BE MADE AND WHY IT IS IMPORTANT

Although you will have chosen up to four changes, you will need to consider the steps for each of the changes that you intend to make. Figure 10.1 (page 146) is a template that you could use for planning one data-informed change process.

First, at the top of the figure, you will need to name the change that you intend to make and outline why this change is important. Remember, always start with your why; putting this at the top of your planning template brings your team back to this core vision and purpose. You have spent a lot of time and effort in thinking about the data and potential practical steps, so this is a good opportunity to return to why you started this process in the first place.

Following this, consider the way you will measure the change, or how you will know you have been successful. As this is a data-informed change process, the goal is to see a change in the data or the outputs in the future. What are you aiming for? What do you hope will improve? Set a realistic and achievable goal for what you are working

We will know we've been successful in this change process when:				
Step number and description	Reason for the step	Communication required (Who and how?)	Staff involved	Completed by (date)
Step 1:				
Step 2:				
Step 3:				
Step 4:				

Figure 10.1: Template for planning for the steps of the change process.

toward and name it on the template. If a SMART goal would be helpful at this point, I encourage you to use that structure. Your focus should be on answering the question, What will the data say when you evaluate this area in the future?

Next, it is important that you consider all the smaller steps required to make the larger change, and the order in which these steps need to occur. When thinking about the steps, consider the following.

- Are any checking or permissions needed before the change process starts?
- How will people learn about each step of the change and when?
- What are the small steps that need to occur to achieve the larger change?
- In what order do the small steps need to occur?
- Which staff will be involved in the steps (senior and middle leaders and recipients)?
- When do you hope to have each step completed by?

By following this process and planning for change with your team, you can unpack the finer details of the change and ensure you cover more bases. Things will always arise to affect the change process that you could never have anticipated, but the more decisions you make at this point, the more easily you will be able to adapt to unanticipated external factors as the change is occurring.

It is vital that you communicate the changes to key stakeholder groups that your change will affect, so deliberately planning communication around each step is important. At no stage should staff either in your team or in the broader school community say that they were unaware a particular step was occurring. Therefore, by outlining the communication strategy and listing the staff who will be involved and at what point, you are identifying who is responsible for communicating with the staff at each stage of the process. Also, remember that telling staff about the change process once is not going to be sufficient—you need to be talking about the data, the change, and the small steps of change regularly.

Assigning a completion date for each small step makes the larger change more attainable, rather than leaving you with a large-scale change to make with a looming deadline. It also holds your team accountable for the incremental steps along the way and ensures that your change agenda stays on track. Regarding the timeline, it is understandable that unforeseen events arise that mean steps do not occur when expected. You need to walk the fine line between prioritizing the change process and adjusting to any unforeseen circumstances. Where possible, adhere to your deadlines and hold the team accountable if they are not met (lean into those potentially difficult conversations with love and vulnerability!), but be adaptable to things that could arise during the change process and willing to modify the plan as you progress.

PRIMING THE ENVIRONMENT BY LEADING UP AND DOWN

> *It doesn't make sense to hire smart people and then tell them what to do; we hire smart people so they can tell us what to do.*
> —*Steve Jobs*

Different staff will each have a different understanding of the usefulness of data in schools, and that is absolutely OK. But no matter what your role is, as a leader, you will need to lead those who are in positions both above and below you, particularly through this impending change. A lot of the discussion up to this point has been specifically about leading your teams, but it is also important that you consider the role you play in leading those above you in the organizational hierarchy as well.

Professional trust is a key element of successful leadership. Whether or not you feel it at all times, you were offered your current job because the people who interviewed you (and those above you) trusted that you could do it. Theoretically, you are in a good position to lead those above and below you in the organizational hierarchy.

But difficulty can lie in people's egos interfering and your skills or vision being more refined in this particular area than those of the people above you.

> One of the most difficult challenges I have experienced is that of timetabling as there are several stakeholders to be served. The stakeholders are the system, the principal, the middle leaders, and staff. All have legitimate claims on the timetable structure, and the serving of each one fairly and with equity is a juggling act—not all will feel they have been treated fairly or equitably. The juggling act is best managed through timely communication with those above and below, and communicating how the decisions will impact all. It is important to emphasize a well-articulated bigger picture, rather than smaller, more selfish individual interests.
> —Terry O'Connor, former head of campus

Given that in many schools the data-informed leadership strategies used are either rare or self-taught, you may find yourself in a position where you have some better skills, or you are building skills and strategies at a quicker rate than the people who put you in the role in the first place. That is OK, but you need to be acutely aware of this situation and of the fact that you need to lead them through the change process too.

In many ways, leading those above us is harder. Yes, we might be trusted to perform our role, but that does not mean that our leaders like us challenging the way they think or reimagining the organizational structures and processes already in place—even though many of them may have been devised prior to the shift toward being data-informed. Often, making changes to and shifting the perspectives of those above us require proposals and thinking time. You need to be proactive and explicit about the ways in which you lead these people and constantly remind yourself that only about 30 percent of employees are using data analytics to their potential in the workplace (Fleming et al., 2019)!

AN EXAMPLE OF LEADING UP AND DOWN

When I was in a middle leadership role that focused on student data and performance in 2016, my leadership team knew that they needed that role but did not necessarily know what it should look like or even what they *wanted* it to look like. I felt like much of my role oscillated between trying to persuade my leadership team to try new approaches or show them different ways of looking at the data, and leading my team of curriculum leaders and building the data literacy of the teaching staff.

One instance that comes to mind in my attempt to influence my leadership team was around the introduction of data walls. Despite the fact that I was in a role that was focused on student data and performance, and despite attempting to use best practice and being informed by research, the senior leadership team in the school did not want data walls—in fact, they philosophically and fundamentally disagreed with the use of them. Their arguments against data walls were largely associated with student privacy—what if a visitor to the school saw the data on the data wall? Shouldn't it be private? What if someone comes to the school at night for debating and sees the students' faces ranked on a wall? In addition to privacy, they had great concerns about a student's reaction if he or she saw him- or herself on a data wall. Both of these arguments and the beliefs of my leaders meant that I was told we would not be having data walls in our school.

> I demonstrate trust in my teams and staff by letting them do their work. A previous colleague once said to me, "Employ good people and let them do their job!" I have good people with well-developed skill sets, so I want them to have the confidence to make decisions and create actions and initiatives that will support our purpose.
> —Wayne Chapman, Principal

Consequently, I needed to lead up as well as lead my team. I had to present the evidence to the leadership team to shift their perceptions, as well as pre-empt and address any concerns that they had. I had to ask what they would allow and then negotiate options they would approve of that would still be effective. In this particular case, it was slow going. I was encouraged to trial my ideas with specific departments in areas of the school where there was no risk of anyone else seeing the data. But once heads of curriculum began sharing stories of student improvement and engagement with the data walls with others, the initiative gained some momentum and the staff implemented more data walls.

As a leader, you need to be able to lead up and lead down. This could take the form of working with your senior leaders, area supervisors, or executive directors, and it requires you to be persuasive and able to negotiate and demonstrate your ability to lead change for those above, around, and below you in the organizational hierarchy, no matter what role you are in. Walk gently when leading up, and use your skills in negotiation as best you can. Ultimately, the hard truth is that if your leaders say no to an idea or initiative you propose, unfortunately there is not much you can do about it. So, set yourself up for success by understanding the research, knowing the people in the team above you, and considering alternate options and conditions to negotiate rather than accepting a *no* as soon as you get one.

PRIMING THE ENVIRONMENT BY BUILDING A CULTURE OF PREDICTING RESULTS

> *We should not pick the most dramatic estimates and show a worst-case scenario as if it were certain. People would find out! We should ideally show a mid-forecast, and also a range of alternative possibilities, from best to worst. If we have to round the numbers, we should round to our own disadvantage. This protects our reputations and means we never give people a reason to stop listening.*
> —Dr. Hans Rosling

While other employment sectors predict, for example, the number of units to manufacture based on previous sales or the number of clients and associated staffing requirements and income, predicting results in schools is, in my opinion, massively underutilized. In the school context, predicting results occurs when educators use summative or formative results to forecast future performance or achievement.

Using data to predict future performance means that educators can guide students toward their most appropriate pathways and assist students with tracking their progress and goal setting. They can identify and address any areas of concern before summative assessments, and schools can anticipate individual student and cohort results in high-stakes, external, or standardized testing so that there are fewer surprises when the results are released. I truly believe that we can handle less-than-pleasing results if we have predicted and tried to address them beforehand.

Predicting grades in schools can take a number of different forms, including the following.

- Using results from formative mock exams to predict students' performances in the final examination. You may do this for senior subjects in which there is a culminating external examination, or where there is a standardized test that you intend to track.

- Building profiles of learners throughout their course of study to predict overall end grades for individual senior subjects. In this instance, you can use the notion of formative work to predict summative results, but when a summative task is completed, this result replaces the prediction. The profiles continue to build over time with a combination of completed summative task results and formative mock task results.

- Using in-class quizzes with a grading scale to indicate to students the level of achievement that they are working at, and connecting this conversation to the way they are moving toward their goals in the subject.

- Having conversations with students about the standard of their work as they are progressing, particularly in practical subjects where comments such as "to demonstrate a higher level, you should work on refining . . ." lead to conversations about anticipated performance grades.

- Mapping tertiary entrance scores backward to learning area results and individual assessment scores to help students work toward a particular benchmark for university entrance. While this requires help from someone who understands the entrance ranking calculations and the weighting of learning areas, it can be useful for students to see what they require in different learning areas to achieve their goals.

- Observing the students' current work rate and the anticipated time required to complete the course to predict module or competency completion.

In all instances, the weighting that you allocate to each piece of formative assessment must be reflective of the overall assessment requirements, and the instrument conditions, content, and structure should be as authentic and similar to the real task as possible.

AN EXAMPLE OF PREDICTING RESULTS

As head of physical education (PE) in south London, I predicted grades regularly to understand my students' performance and provide feedback to support their goals, self-reflection, and self-monitoring. When I was in this role, General Certificate of Secondary Education (GCSE) PE results were calculated based on a combination of practical and theoretical results, with 50 percent of the overall grade being the final external theory assessment. The 50 percent practical result was a combination of a written task and four individual sport results, where each student's best four sports were used to calculate the overall grade.

When I started in this role, only 26 percent of the previous cohort had passed the subject. So, I began predicting the grades for students to help get as many as possible into the C category and above. In almost every lesson, I displayed a spreadsheet that documented all the sports that the students had results for, selected the best results, and then combined their practical results with their achievement in formative mock external assessments (see figure 10.2, page 152, for the shaded spreadsheet. For a color-coded version of this figure, visit **go.SolutionTree.com/leadership**). I regularly gave students sections of previous external exams so that I could see the areas of low achievement and areas on which I should focus my teaching and revision. I added

GRADE 11 GCSE PE CURRENT GRADES 5

	Target	Athletics	Badminton	Basketball	Fitness	Football	Tennis	Swimming	Trampolining	Judo	Dance	Netball	Softball	Skiing	Prac mark out of 40	Analysis task 10%	C/work total % predicted	C/work predicted grade	Exam predicted	Overall predicted %	Overall predicted grade
Student 1	B	3	7	6	3	6						8	7		28	7	70.0	C	46	66.5	D
Student 2	A	7	9	7	8	7			6	8			9	8	34	8	84.2	A	51	77.7	B
Student 3	A	3	7	10	0	4			7			9	7		33	9.5	84.6	A	52	78.5	A
Student 4	A	6	6	5	8	6		8	6	8				10	34	9	85.8	A	51	78.7	A
Student 5	B	7	8	7	4	7			5	7			6		29	7	72.1	B	50	69.9	C
Student 6	D	6	7	4	6	7			4						26	6	65.2	D	30	54.5	D
Student 7	C	2	6	4	5	6				8					25	6.5	62.9	D	23	50.0	E
Student 8	A	8	7	6	9	7				8			7		32	9	81.7	A	46	73.5	B
Student 9	C	5	5	5	6	6	6		7		10	7	7		31	6	74.6	B	30	60.8	D
Student 10	C	6	7	5	9	5			8			8	6		32	8	80.0	A	45	72.0	C
Student 11	C	3	5	4	4	4			7			6	5		23	5	56.3	D	32	50.8	E
Student 12	A*	9	7	8	8	10	8			10			7		37	9	92.1	A*	39	76.1	B
Student 13	B	7	6	8	4	7			7		10				30	7	74.2	B	40	65.8	D
Student 14	B	7	7	8	9	10						6	9		36	9	90.0	A*	28	68.9	C
Student 15	C	3	7	5	0	4			6				6		25	5	60.4	D	26	50.1	E
Student 16	B	5	7	6	6	6			5				6		25	6	62.1	D	49	63.4	D
Student 17	A*	8	9	6	6	8			7			6	8		33	8	82.1	A	54	78.1	A
Student 18	C	7	7	8	0	6			6				8		30	7	74.2	B	36	63.7	D
Student 19	D	4	5	6	0	7			4				6		24	5	58.3	D	8	39.3	F
Numbers		4	14	5	14	11	1	1	6	4	2	6	12	2			A*-C / A*-A	68 42 / 42 11		A*-C / A*-A	47 37 / 21 05

Figure 10.2: An example of a predicted grades spreadsheet.

practical scores as they achieved them and then highlighted their top four sports in green (shown in figure 10.2 as dark grey)—indicating that they would count toward their overall GCSE grade. As I targeted my revision and intervention sessions for the topics they needed to work on (shown in figure 10.2 as light grey), their results slowly improved, and the percentage of students predicted at a C or above began to rise.

The spreadsheet became a key talking point in my senior PE class. I updated practical results as we did further assessments, and celebrated with students when they moved up a predicted grade. Over time, students could see the impact of increasing their marks in the practical activities and in adding different sport options, as well as the effect of additional study and work on the theory component of the subject. In lessons where I needed to emphasize the importance of students engaging in the learning and content in a particular area, I referred to their goals on the spreadsheet and the difference between them and their current working grades.

Inside and outside class, students in my senior PE class often approached me and asked to modify or change the spreadsheet to see if raising certain results would make a difference overall. Students would tinker with small improvements in a number of areas against a big improvement in another area to see the impact it would have on their overall prediction. These conversations led to discussions about what was easiest to make small improvements in—were they close to the next level in a practical activity, or could they be assessed by their coach at their weekly game in a different sport to improve their overall result?

My goal in this role was to achieve a 50 percent pass rate in my first year—something my predictions indicated was a long way off at the beginning of the year but that became more and more likely as the year progressed. I was trying my hardest and doing everything I could for my students, and the data along the way affirmed that students were making improvements. Thankfully, my predictions worked, and we achieved a 52 percent pass rate in my first year, which went much higher again in my second! I have no doubt that forecasting played a major part in the improvements, and I couldn't believe that schools were not doing similar things when I returned to Australia.

Predicting grades and sharing our predictions with students help build students' metacognition around their learning and performance and increase motivation. When I talked about the importance of transparency in step 3 (page 77), I related an example in which I predicted Queensland Core Skills (QCS) test grades for my grade 12 students and worked with the school captain and his peers. An example of the way in which I predicted their grades based on mock exams can be seen in figure 10.3 (page 154). In this figure, the dark grey shading represents high scores, the medium grey shading represents scores in need of improvement, and the light grey shading represents low

BEST PRACTICE RESULTS

Student name	Latest test date	Writing	Writing grade	Test Date	SRI	SRI Grade	Test Date	MCQ	MCQ grade	AVERAGE SCORE	PREDICTED QCS GRADE
Student 1	August	3+	C	August	45.5	B	APR-18	54%	C	3.25	C
Student 2	Term 1, 2016	2-	B	August	28.5	D	August	56%	C	3	C
Student 3	August	3	C	August	44	B	August	66%	B	3.75	B
Student 4	July	2-	B	August	42	B	August	72%	B	4	B
Student 5	July	3	C	August	38.5	C	August	66%	B	3.5	C
Student 6	August	2-	B	May	30.5	D	August	58%	C	3	C
Student 7	August	2-	B	May	33	C	August	50%	C	3.25	C
Student 8	August	2	B	April	42	B	Term 4, 2015	80%	A	4.5	B
Student 9	August	3+	C	August	34.5	C	August	70%	B	3.5	C
Student 10	August	2-	B	May	27	D	August	60%	C	3	C
Student 11	Term 4, 2015	3+	C	April	35.5	C	Term 4, 2015	78%	B	3.5	C
Student 12	August	3+	C	August	41	B	August	84%	A	4.25	B
Student 13	August	2	B	August	35	C	August	56%	C	3.25	C
Student 14	August	2+	B	May	43	B	August	54%	C	3.5	C
Student 15	Term 4, 2015	2-	B	August	30	C	August	64%	C	3.25	C
Student 16	August	2-	B	August	30	C	August	50%	C	3.25	C
Student 17	August	3+	C	May	22.5	D	Term 4, 2015	44%	D	2.25	D
Student 18	August	3	C	August	38.5	C	Term 4, 2015	66%	B	3.5	C
Student 19	August	3	C	April	30.5	C	Term 4, 2015	58%	C	3	C
Student 20	August	2	B	May	45.5	B	August	62%	C	3.5	C
Student 21	July	2+	B	August	34	C	August	50%	C	3.25	C
Student 22	August	2+	B	August	46	B	Term 4, 2015	86%	A	4.5	B
Student 23	August	2	B	Term 4, 2015	44.5	B	August	72%	B	4	B
Student 24	August	3+	C	Term 4, 2015	42	B	August	74%	B	3.75	B

Figure 10.3: An example of the way I predicted QCS test grades for grade 12 students.

scores in need of much improvement. Visit **go.SolutionTree.com/leadership** for a color-coded version of this figure.

Predicting grades is particularly useful because it removes some of the guessing and estimation when both you and your students want to make improvements. Effective teaching practices are obviously the most important factor in improving educational outcomes, but when the stakeholders can do something about the results, being able to measure and predict the impact that different approaches are having throughout the process is invaluable. But the ways in which you collect data must, as much as possible, replicate the actual assessment type and conditions. Otherwise your data will not provide a valid comparison for the purpose of predicting results.

I strongly encourage you to consider the ways in which you could use predictions with and for the teams that you are leading, and throughout your change process. There is no point setting a target of doubling a pass rate in a particular learning area and then not measuring your progress toward the goal during the year. Why wait until the end of the year to see whether you have achieved your goal?

KEY SUMMARY

- Step 8 of the change process requires you to create your action plan for change. Consider the small steps that are required, the people involved, the communication strategy, and the expected timeline of each step.

- If you are able to manage the challenge of leading up and down, you will be able to have an impact and influence in your setting. Without this skill, any attempt at change will be ineffective. When leading up, use research to support your negotiations, pre-empt the issues that your leaders might identify and formulate responses to their possible issues, and attempt to identify solutions. Be prepared to accommodate their concerns and make some movement toward their views, but walk the fine line between persisting with your goals and negotiating.

- Walk gently. If you are leading up, they still get the final say, but try to influence them nicely!

- Don't take a hard no—keep trying and offering options. See whether you can trial the idea with a smaller group or department and whether it is successful there first.

- Predicting results and future achievement develops a level of certainty about the impact of the change process.

- Tracking and predicting impact and outcomes throughout the change process allows you to modify your approach if and when it is required.

- Predict results wherever possible with students and staff. Predicting results builds metacognition around the goals and improvement and increases motivation of staff and students.

- Ensure the tasks that you use to predict results mimic the final assessment conditions as much as possible. The closer you get to replicating the content, skills, and question types, the more accurate your predictions will be.

REFLECTION QUESTIONS

During the process of analyzing an action plan for your work, use the following questions to reflect on the progress you and your team are making.

- How will you utilize the planning template?

- Will your whole team work through and contribute to one planning template at a time, or will you have two, three, or four groups of staff write a plan for one change process?

- If you have smaller teams, with each working on one planning template, how will you seek the wisdom of the larger group? Will they present their ideas? Will everyone have the opportunity to contribute to every plan?

- What factors will affect the timing and logistics of your steps for action?

- How can you encourage team members to set realistic time goals?

- How can you ensure team members adhere to the time goals?

- How much leading up do you currently do?

- How do you cope when you hit roadblocks dealing with people above you in the organizational hierarchy?

- How can you improve the way in which you manage these challenges?

- Whom could you approach to seek further advice about these challenges?

chapter eleven

MAKE THE CHANGE

The penultimate step of this process is to implement the change plan. At this stage, you have a well-planned series of steps, you know who in the team is responsible for which parts of the plan, and you know when the change and the smaller steps should be occurring. Throughout the process of making the change, check in regularly with your team, get progress reports, work through challenges, be flexible, and adapt where necessary.

This step takes the most time and is the hardest to navigate. Some research has found that over 70 percent of significant change efforts fail (Kotter, 1996)—aim to be in the 30 percent of change efforts that succeed! The final two aspects of priming the environment are particularly important during step 9, and they are (1) reaching a critical mass or tipping point and (2) celebrating small wins.

PRIMING THE ENVIRONMENT BY REACHING A CRITICAL MASS OR TIPPING POINT

> *Everyone needs to see the followers, because new followers emulate followers—not the leader.*
> —Derek Sivers

At this stage of the process, you are trying to lead change with a larger group of teachers and staff, but true change will not occur until you reach a critical mass, or tipping point, with the percentage of your staff that is on board.

In the field of leadership, there is a significant amount of research and reading available on creating a movement. Derek Sivers (2010) offers a wonderful analogy of leading change, from being an easy-to-follow individual with an idea to getting that first follower to reaching a critical mass and eventually leading a movement. Sivers (2010) narrates footage of a man dancing by himself at a music event before other dancers slowly join him:

> Now here come two more, then three more. Now we've got momentum. This is the tipping point! Now we've got a movement! As more people jump in, it's no longer risky. If they were on the fence before, there's no reason not to join now. They won't be ridiculed, they won't stand out, and they will be part of the in-crowd, if they hurry.

This analogy illustrates the power of one person taking a risk and slowly recruiting others on the journey to create a movement.

The tipping point, or critical mass, is the point at which a number of your followers can lead significant change. When the number reaches this point, the new ideas, approaches, or processes involved in the change begin to take over, and the change starts to take effect. Leading change as an individual is almost always impossible, but by recruiting people who believe in your vision and support the change process, your followers begin to recruit others, those who have been recruited start to recruit, and, before long, you are no longer the only dancing guy trying to lead change. You end up with a team of people around you on the same mission, who feel as if they are part of the in-crowd and who advocate for and enable the change to happen.

The mythical critical mass regularly mentioned in the literature is the percentage of your organization that is required to be on board in order for change to occur and have an impact. Research in this area differs, but it is generally reported that a relatively small number of people—somewhere between 10 to 30 percent of the organization—is required to hit the critical mass (see Gladwell, 2006; Oliver, Marwell, & Teixeira, 1985; Swiss, Fallon, & Burgos, 2012). Once this point is reached, as Sivers (2010) states, people begin to follow the followers rather than solely the initial leader, and the change begins to snowball.

The notion of a critical mass is relevant for leading change in schools more broadly, as well as in smaller teams. As the leader, you need to aim and work out how to get 10 to 30 percent of your staff on board with your initial change agenda or data-informed processes. The way in which you achieve this will vary depending on your situation and the context and climate of your organization. Sometimes staff will come along quickly and willingly as first adopters, as they understand your why and see the benefits of the vision (this is certainly more likely to happen when your school environment is primed for change). But others will require more work and may even need you to reach out to them specifically to provide direction or guidance in becoming part of your team leading change.

The easiest way to build these numbers in the early days of your project is to work with a guiding coalition of staff who understand the vision—in this case, your data or project team. If you can recruit key people early in this process, they will have done much of the heavy lifting for you by this point and already begun to recruit others by going back to their classrooms and trying new things or talking to their colleagues about the project. Other teachers in your school will start to follow your followers instead of following you. That is where the power of the critical mass lies.

THE WILLINGNESS AND ABILITY OF STAFF

Other than the people who join your team early and enthusiastically, there might be those who you know have potential but who do not put themselves out there openly to support you. Sometimes they may not be convinced that they have the skills necessary, and so they might just need that little bit of extra encouragement to be involved. By reaching out to them, you are demonstrating that you trust their judgment, respect the work that they are doing, and see their potential and the role they could be playing in the school.

AN EXAMPLE OF BUILDING A CRITICAL MASS

One curriculum leader whom I worked with in a previous school was keen to adopt data-informed practices, as he knew a lot about my passion for using data well and was incredibly supportive of my vision. But he was also honest about the fact that he did not really know where to start in his department and did not have the knowledge or the skills to implement any data-informed practices to lead change.

Although he didn't necessarily have the skill, I saw him as a potential early adopter because of his desire to be involved. I approached him and asked if I could trial some strategies in his department and show him some things that might work. He was enthusiastic to do so, partly because he saw the value in it but also because he wanted to be the first department to adopt the new practices. While there was genuine interest on his part, he also realized that it would be beneficial for him to be learning new skills and trialing new approaches that he could then share with others. As a result, I worked with him to implement a host of tracking processes, including data walls that showed both progress and achievement in his learning area and individual teacher tracking sheets.

Because of the work he was doing as a leader and teacher in his learning area, other teachers in his department became curious about the change and asked about his approaches and processes. The curriculum leader ended up becoming my main advocate for the data-informed processes, and he regularly engaged in conversations with members of his team and other curriculum leaders. Because his team could see the value of the processes through his lens, they began to trial the processes too. Consequently, he began spending more time on and with the data at department meetings, and teachers in his department began regularly discussing data and performance with him and with their students.

As more data-informed conversations opened up between teachers and students, students began to approach the middle leader and his teachers for further feedback on their growth and achievement. With more student buy-in, the teachers were motivated to continue and establish ways of working with data. Consequently, two months into the change process, the curriculum leader was able to report on the processes of his department to the rest of the staff, his department team had witnessed the benefits of the changes through their department, and other curriculum leaders were keen to jump on board and embrace the change.

SKILL VERSUS WILL

This story of the curriculum leader and his data journey is a timely reminder of the skill-versus-will matrix that regularly appears in leadership literature, as shown in figure 11.1.

All employees sit somewhere in the matrix relative to the two axes, from low to high skill (vertical axis) and from low to high will (horizontal axis). Each employee's position on the vertical axis (skill) is dependent on his or her ability to do the role that he or she is in. The employee's position on the horizontal axis (will) relates to the motivation that he or she has for his or her role, as well as the desire that he or she has to learn and do a good job. Although the image represents four quadrants that employees fit into, both axes are a continuum. Therefore, staff could be positioned at any point

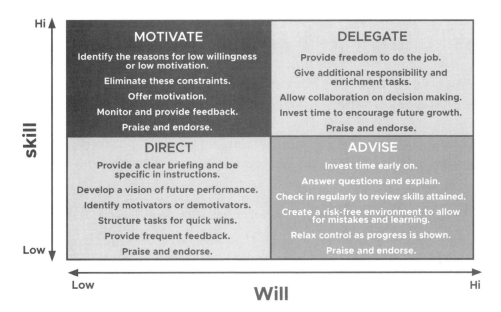

Source: *Adapted from Landsberg, 2003.*
Figure 11.1: Skill-versus-will matrix.

in any box. The four quadrants of this matrix, and therefore the four broad categories that employees could fall into, are:

- High skill, high will
- High skill, low will
- Low skill, high will
- Low skill, low will

Although employees can be positioned anywhere within these four categories, and each employee is unique, there are some generalizations that we can make about staff depending on their position within the four quadrants of this matrix. High skill and high will employees are great to have on staff. Low skill and high will employees persist and work with you to improve and therefore are key staff. But high skill–low will and low skill–low will staff make change incredibly difficult, and on the off chance that these classifications are coupled with a negative or fixed mindset, these individuals can also derail your improvement efforts.

An employee with high skill and high will is generally motivated, enthusiastic, and keen to adopt new things in an organization. People in this category look for additional challenges and opportunities to grow and develop. From a coaching perspective, the employees in the delegate category should be encouraged to be involved in decision-making processes and provided with additional responsibilities and opportunities. This will show these employees that you respect their work, trust their judgment, and recognize their potential.

High skill and low will employees are often those with a lot of experience but who may have plateaued. They may be disillusioned with the organization or leadership, and despite having the skills to do a good job, they may choose not to. High skill and low will employees are in the motivate category, as you need to tap into their motivation and provide an environment that inspires them to buy into the process. This might require you to find out directly what would motivate them and provide both intrinsic motivation and extrinsic rewards, but the effort can be worthwhile. If you manage to have this type of employee buy-in, you will shift them into the high skill–high will category.

Low skill and high will employees are those with the desire and motivation to do a particular job but who may lack the necessary skills, such as staff who are new to their role. These individuals fit into the advise category, as the best thing that you can do as a leader is support them, provide them with additional training to learn necessary skills, capitalize on teachable moments, provide them with feedback, and encourage them to persist. This will show these employees that you believe they can improve and that you recognize they are trying hard to do so. These individuals are generally motivated to do well and, with training, will easily move into the high skill–high will category.

Employees who are low skill and low will are troublesome, because while you can offer training to improve their skill, it may be hard to motivate them and raise their willingness to do the task. Employees in the direct category are sometimes given jobs that they do not enjoy or did not request or can be new or young staff who are still learning but are also afraid to take risks and fail. These employees require clear direction and clarity around the quality of work that you expect and the additional training that they require, but working with staff who have low motivation to change can be difficult. You may need to remove barriers and identify intrinsic motivators and extrinsic rewards to inspire them. While this situation is difficult to navigate, if you are authentic about your desire to make improvements and learn about the needs of your employees, you are far more likely to succeed.

THE SKILL-VERSUS-WILL FRAMEWORK IN DATA-INFORMED CHANGE

From the perspective of data-informed change, the skill-versus-will model is a useful way to categorize the employees in your organization and the way in which you will build your guiding coalition and critical mass. It would be pointless to try building your guiding coalition with employees who have low skill and low will—your first adopters need to be your high skill–high will employees. They will work well for you as the leader, and this also provides them with a challenge that they may be looking for.

As the size of the group supporting the change process increases, focus on staff with low skill but high will next. Like my example of the curriculum leader, someone who is enthusiastic and keen to learn is great to work with. Such employees' skills can always be improved, and if they have high motivation to begin with, you are more than halfway there.

It would be fruitless to invest a lot of time early on in low skill and low will employees, as they are far less likely to buy into the change process at this point, or at all. Get some quick wins early, build your critical mass, and then begin the hard work with those employees who need additional inspiration and training.

ALIGNMENT WITH KOTTER'S CHANGE PROCESS

In Kotter's eight steps of leading change (see figure 2.1, page 33), step 2 (build a guiding coalition) and step 4 (enlist a volunteer army) both speak to the notion of building a critical mass of followers who are supportive of and aligned with your vision.

Step 2 calls on the leader to recruit highly effective people from within the ranks who can guide, lead, and communicate the vision of the change team. These people become your data or change team and are classified as your early adopters or first followers. Generally, these will be your high skill–high will staff members.

In step 4, enlisting the volunteer army relies on members of your guiding coalition going out and spreading the message and advocating for change to the masses. This is where the message is communicated to the broader organization and where it is essential that all members of your guiding coalition have bought in and can see the importance of having a sense of urgency around the change. This is a great opportunity to involve the low skill–high will staff who you (or your high skill–high will staff) can upskill to bring them along on the change journey with you.

At step 10 of this change process (see chapter 12, page 169), you need to consider the ways in which you can use this notion of a critical mass to leverage your reform and change efforts. While there will always be people who may not agree with the changes, or those whom you will struggle to get onside, 10 to 30 percent is achievable in any context. Without achieving the critical mass, your change efforts are likely to fall flat. Remember, although through this process you are handing over some of the heavy lifting to your guiding coalition, the people you find difficult to engage may end up coming on board because they follow their colleagues, not you.

PRIMING THE ENVIRONMENT BY CELEBRATING SMALL WINS

> *It is still much easier to coach people to fit in. It is still much easier to reward people when they say something that you were going to say, as opposed to rewarding people when they say something entirely different than what you were going to say. But when we . . . figure out how to celebrate difference and how to let people bring the best version of themselves forward, well . . . that is the world I want my sons to grow up in.*
> —Frances Frei

Assuming that you have set up a data team, you are being transparent with the data and are talking about it regularly, you are embracing vulnerability and authenticity, you are constantly reminding people of the why, your guiding coalition has helped build the critical mass, and you are seeing small shifts in practice, then you are leading great, data-informed change in your school that aligns with your original vision and goals.

If this is you, or more importantly if it *isn't*, you need to consider the way in which you will celebrate small wins to highlight the people who are doing the good work, making progress, and persisting with the change efforts. Celebrating small wins at any stage of the process encourages the staff member who has made the change, reminds other staff of the expectations and the goals of the work, and shows your staff that you value their contributions and see the good they are doing in their departments or classrooms.

ALIGNMENT WITH KOTTER'S CHANGE PROCESS

John Kotter refers to celebrating small wins in step 6 of his eight-step process for leading change (generate short-term wins). In fact, Kotter states, "Wins are the molecules of results. They must be recognized, collected and communicated—early and often—to track progress and energise volunteers to persist" (Kotter, n.d.). Sometimes, the little bit of encouragement that celebrating short-term wins can have will spur people on, or it may motivate another team member to start trying.

In my experience of leading change in a number of contexts, I found generating short-term wins to be a key element of shifting school communities to being data-informed communities. Leading change is hard, and sometimes it feels like there is more going wrong than right. But it is important to look for the positives and celebrate the small wins when you find them.

There are a few ways I have used this principle in leading school change, and in how I have seen it have an impact on the organizational culture. Firstly, recognizing small wins is morale boosting for yourself and others—it is a (sometimes) timely reminder that positive change is happening. Remember, negativity dominance can take over at times, and people can focus on the reasons why a change is not working. Don't let it get you (or your teachers) down. Remind them of the good things by celebrating small achievements authentically and in a timely manner.

Secondly, I have asked teachers who implemented an idea in their classroom or who have seen growth in their learning area to share their approaches and learnings with staff, providing an opportunity for them to lead a professional development session for their peers. The first time I did this, Heath, a PE teacher who was initially undecided as to whether he'd engage with the use of tracking processes, got up in front of the teaching staff and talked about the positive impact they were having in his classes. This was a great opportunity for him to present his work to his peers, and it showed the whole staff more of him than they would have normally seen, particularly in this data-informed realm.

Lastly, publicizing small wins shows other staff in the team the progress that is being made, and it motivates them to change as well. When Heath got up and spoke about data, the rest of his PE team didn't know what he'd been doing in his classes. They looked at his approach with fresh eyes and could immediately see the connection to their learning area and classrooms. Because they respected Heath, they saw the link between his use of tracking processes and the improvements he was making in their learning area more clearly than I ever would have been able to demonstrate. The pedagogy in the entire department improved because Heath shared his practice with the teaching staff.

SCHOOL LEADERS' REFLECTIONS ON CELEBRATING SMALL WINS

I asked two school leaders about their perceptions on the importance of celebrating small wins. Former school and system leader Catherine Jackson stated:

> Our brains are tuned to look for problems and threats—it's a natural survival instinct, but it doesn't necessarily serve us well. It also means that to tune into the bright spots, to tune into successes, to be aware of small wins and celebrate along the way, requires very intentional effort. The bad stuff will get noticed easily. The good stuff needs to get noticed and celebrated. And it's the role of the leader to do that. (C. Jackson, personal communication, June 24, 2019)

How right she is. In every 360-degree review, observation of my teaching, and review of a workshop or presentation that I have led, I have always looked to the elements that weren't as good as the others! Of course, we should all be learning from our feedback, but that negativity dominance occasionally bites us when it shouldn't. In another interview, principal Wayne Chapman stated:

> I think that we are highly critical in nature as a profession. As such we habitually criticize our own work and the work of others. This, combined with the busyness of school life, means we tend to focus on what we could have done better or simply jump ahead to the next issue, event, or program, instead of stopping, taking in the view, and enjoying that success. Celebration is a key part of the change process. Naming and celebration of the small wins are vital in adding impetus to change. Big wins should lead to big celebrations. (W. Chapman, personal communication, June 19, 2019)

As can be seen in both of these responses, Catherine and Wayne recognize the importance of celebrating successes and small wins in a school. Although leadership literature tells us about the importance of doing so, their reflections on negativity bias show that this is an important consideration for leaders, and it is something that we need to do more often in our schools.

CELEBRATING WINS EVEN WHEN PROGRESS IS SLOW

It is still important to celebrate small wins even when things are not going to plan, but this can be a difficult road to walk. If negativity dominance is affecting you or your team, you need to ensure that your recognition of good news stories is authentic. (Remember to ensure you demonstrate rigor in your logic to consciously build trust.)

If your team thinks that the metaphorical building is burning down around them and you are grasping at straws to find something to celebrate, you will lose their respect. They will question whether you know what is happening in the organization and question your leadership. So, it is important that you are transparent about the fact that some things are not going well, but that you still believe it is important to recognize the good bits. If done well and authentically, this has the potential to motivate your team members and reorient them toward the goal.

KEY SUMMARY

- Step 9 is where you get to make the change!
- Reaching the critical mass will lead to action and change. Without it, you will not have enough staff working with the change project to build momentum and you will fail to create action.
- Aim to reach the 10 to 30 percent critical mass as soon as you can.
- Identify people who can and will be a part of your guiding coalition and therefore your critical mass. If they show skill or will in the area, encourage their involvement.
- Remember that some people in your organization will follow your followers, and that's OK. Your guiding coalition will help reach more people in your organization, and this is actually more likely to build your change efforts, not derail them.
- Build your critical mass by considering where your staff lie in the skill-versus-will matrix. Start with those who are high skill–high will and work with the low skill–high will employees for some quick wins and to build your critical mass.
- Celebrating small wins when they occur means that staff are recognized and valued. If this isn't done, it can lead to a culture of disengagement and apathy. If their efforts and improvements aren't being recognized, why should (and would) staff continue trying?
- Be positive. Look for the great things that are happening and celebrate them as often as possible.

- Recognize the staff who are making changes and working to achieve your vision, no matter how small, and recognize their efforts both privately and publicly.

- Your recognition of the small wins must be authentic and done in a timely manner for it to have a positive impact.

- Public recognition has the potential to boost morale, motivate others, and reaffirm that change is possible for you and your team members.

REFLECTION QUESTIONS

Congratulations! You've made it to the point where you are implementing change in your organization. Use the following questions to reflect on the progress you and your team have made.

- Where do your staff sit on the skill-versus-will matrix? Whom would you put in each category, and what percentage of your organization is in each quadrant?

- Think about the individuals in the high skill–high will category—are they involved in your change process? How can you encourage them to be more involved with the project?

- Think about your staff in the low skill–high will category. What do they need from you to move into the high skill–high will category? How can you quickly have them in your change team and leading change themselves?

- Think about the staff whom you have in the high skill–low will category. What do they need from you to increase their motivation? How can you touch base with each of these teachers individually to attempt to remove barriers to their involvement?

- Think about the people who are in the low skill–low will category. How will you approach them? How will you make time to meet with them and support them in the training that they require? How will you best have this conversation with them?

- How do you celebrate small wins in your school, and how can you do it better?

  - Do you celebrate growth and achievement?

  - Do you celebrate staff and student growth and achievement?

  - How do you recognize these wins? In newsletters? At assemblies? In staff meetings?

  - Do you have a mechanism for staff to nominate others to celebrate small achievements?

chapter twelve

EVALUATE THE IMPACT

There is no point investing all the time and effort to make a change up to this point and then never considering the impact that you had once the program was implemented. Similarly, there is no point in initiating a change project that is six months long and not checking in on its progress until its conclusion. As a data-informed leader, you must ensure that you evaluate the change at the end of the project as well as consider all the ways in which you can track the progress you are making along the way.

Whatever your goal is, regularly check in with your team and go back over the data that you are collecting along the way to see whether your project is having an impact. You also need to check in frequently with your key stakeholders to ascertain the impact of the changes and determine whether the project is on track to achieve its desired aims or original goals. Staff are the key to your change effort being successful, so you absolutely must ensure that you are regularly checking in with the people who are doing a lot of the heavy lifting.

If you resolved any issues that arose as you were progressing through the project, or if you have achieved your goal, then well done! You have achieved something that approximately less than 30 percent of change leaders do (Kotter, n.d.)—you have successfully led a team through data-informed change. If this is the case, you will have been celebrating small wins along the way in a way that is authentic and timely. The completion of your project also necessitates that you celebrate the impact you have had and show gratitude to the people who have been involved in the process. Remember, while you might have headed up the change effort, you could not have done it without the team of people around you. Make sure they know that you deeply appreciate the role that they played.

While you should celebrate with your team and show your gratitude for the work that they have put in, you need to think about the next project. Schools are ever evolving, with a myriad of moving parts. There is always going to be an area that is underperforming and that needs your focus or attention. Go back and review your new data with the hope of raising expectations and achievement further, confident in the knowledge that you and your team have the skills to effect positive change, and then find your next project. Imagine the growth your students, staff, and the school as a whole could achieve if you were able to capitalize on regular and effective change cycles.

WHAT HAPPENS IF THE CHANGE PROCESS DOES NOT GO TO PLAN?

If, on the other hand, you do not see adequate improvements during the process and your check-ins along the way indicate that the change process is failing, call your team back together and brainstorm ideas while you are still in the change process.

Don't be afraid to hear from key stakeholders who are affected by the change and take their feedback, and don't worry if you decide to modify your approach or the pre-planned steps. You may need to add more steps, slow down the time between them, involve more or fewer staff, or change the process itself. Remember to conduct small and regular evaluations along the way so that you don't get to the end of the project without any idea that it is going to fail. Choose to do something about the change process while you are in it to maximize the chance of success.

While you might be the leader, you will never have all the answers, and that is OK. Hopefully your entire team is aware of the why and understands the benefit of the change to the school and its students. So, sit with your team, reflect on the progress, utilize their reflective practices, and talk about how you are going to make improvements that lead to change.

If you are monitoring progress throughout the change process but fear that the plan has failed, spend some time with your team reflecting on the process to ascertain what went wrong. Ask questions such as the following.

- Did we target the wrong area?
- Was the analysis or approach influenced by subjective opinion?
- Were the data or the analysis of the data inaccurate?

- Did it become obvious during the process that we should have directed our efforts elsewhere?

- Has something come to light since the project started that indicates there were additional or different issues?

- Were the reasons for the trends in the data not what the team thought they were?

- Was the chosen change option the wrong one? Why or why not?

- What have we learned from the process, and what could we do differently in the future?

- What have we learned since the beginning of the process that has influenced our impact?

Although these questions will support this process, it will be a difficult conversation to have with your team. You are, after all, attempting to have an open discussion about the things that didn't go to plan.

The risk in these types of conversations is that people's egos will affect the flow or progress of the conversation because failure makes us feel vulnerable. Almost all of us, if we care about the job that we do, have a fear that people will judge us for our failings, particularly when we have publicized what our goals are. But by owning it, leading with vulnerability and authenticity, supporting your team, considering alternatives, and seeking the advice of members of your community, you will learn more about the issue and be more likely to succeed next time. Remind people that you did not set out to fail and that you began the process with the right intentions.

Although you and your team might be battered and bruised after a failed change effort, you need to persist. As Greek philosopher Heraclitus of Ephesus said, change is the only constant; this is particularly accurate in schools. If you need help to guide your team in the right direction, don't be afraid to turn to others outside the school—whether they are from another school, from the broader system, or external consultants. There is no shame in asking for help. Lean in with love, embrace that vulnerability, and see it as a learning opportunity for you and your school. When you are clear about your why and the changes that you aim to see for the students in your context, you and your leadership will not be judged negatively. If anything, you will gain more respect for acknowledging that you do not have all the answers and for asking for help.

KEY SUMMARY

- The final step is to evaluate your impact. Did your change process go to plan?

- If it did, well done! Celebrate your achievements, recognize the contribution of the people in your team, and show your gratitude for the time and effort they have invested.

- If your project did not achieve the aims you expected, bring your team back together to talk about the process. Have an open and honest conversation about the strengths and issues with the plan, and map a future plan together.

- If necessary, seek the help of knowledgeable people from other schools or in the broader system, external consultants, or experts.

- Think about the next change process. What will you tackle next? What was on your list to do once the first few changes were made?

REFLECTION QUESTIONS

During the process of reflecting on the impact that your change process had, use the following questions to reflect on the progress you and your team have made.

- What did you learn from this process about leading data-informed change?

- What did you learn about yourself as a leader during this process?

- What skills did you develop throughout this process?

- What skills do you need to continue to develop through future leadership challenges?

- What are some key learnings from this experience that you will take with you into future challenges?

EPILOGUE

> *I'm a very serious "possibilist." That's something I made up. It means someone who neither hopes without reason, nor fears without reason, someone who constantly resists the overdramatic worldview. As a possibilist, I see all this progress, and it fills me with conviction and hope that further progress is possible. This is not optimistic. It is having a clear and reasonable idea about how things are. It is having a worldview that is constructive and useful.*
> —Dr. Hans Rosling

Leadership is changing. No longer are power and hierarchies the order of the day. Instead, horizontal leadership structures where senior leaders learn alongside and with their team members are becoming the norm. This is potentially challenging for leaders who have experienced the former modeled for most of their career and have grown up thinking that these two things are key indicators of success. Instead, leaders who embrace vulnerability and authenticity, prioritize professional trust in their teams, demonstrate a growth and curiosity mindset, are innovative and creative, and celebrate small wins with their teams are those who are increasingly respected, successful, and leading real change in schools across the world.

While the characteristics of effective leadership are changing, so too are the expectations for schools, teachers, and senior leaders to lead with data-informed practices and data-informed decision making. This is challenging for senior and middle leaders who are trying to mediate changing leadership expectations and a changing context with the amount of data that exists in schools. Consequently, much of the leadership, change, and data-informed-practices literature sits separately from one another, and does not consider leadership of data-informed change as a whole. This resource has done just that.

Leading data-informed teams through change is a hard task, even for the most experienced leaders. Working in a context where data are affecting our work and are used as a measure of our effectiveness and the way in which our schools are compared can be daunting. Ultimately, a leader of a data-informed team needs to be confident in his or her ability as a leader first and foremost, and then needs to consider the characteristics that are most likely to prime the environment and support data-informed change to ensure it is effective. Leadership is a tough business, but by considering the characteristics that we bring to the table, we are already examining the best conditions required for our teams and setting them up for success.

At the beginning of this book and throughout the ten-step change process (see page 41), I discussed twelve factors that are required to prime the environment for change (see figure 2.3, page 40). These are elements of school culture and our leadership that we can proactively build throughout this process. Without a primed environment, leaders will find the change process difficult. All twelve of these priming elements are depicted in figure E.1, with the priming elements sitting in the blue ring, the positive cultural outcomes on the outside, and the negative implications and the absence of the characteristic sitting on the inside.

Steps 1 to 10 unpacked the process by which data-informed change could occur in schools. There is much discussion that change efforts are more likely to fail than succeed (Kotter, 1996) and that research on the change process often does not make its way into change in practice in schools (Evidence for Learning, 2019). For these reasons, the ten steps offered in this resource provide a research-based, practical structure that could be followed by a leader attempting to lead data-informed change in schools. It is important that all ten steps are followed in order, and all are given the time and attention that they deserve. If a team were to omit a step, success along the path would be challenging. The ten steps in the change process are depicted in figure 2.4 (page 42).

So, considering the role of the primed environment and the ten-step change process, the two images can be combined so the puzzle pieces fit inside the primed environment. This relationship is depicted in figure E.2 (page 176).

Unprepared, negative, or toxic work environments will never lead to long-term improvement, no matter how visionary, enthusiastic, or skilled the leader is. The change process, in these conditions, is almost certain to fail. And so, we need to demonstrate effective leadership characteristics and prepare the school culture as best we can so that it is receptive to change. When we can do that effectively, we surround the

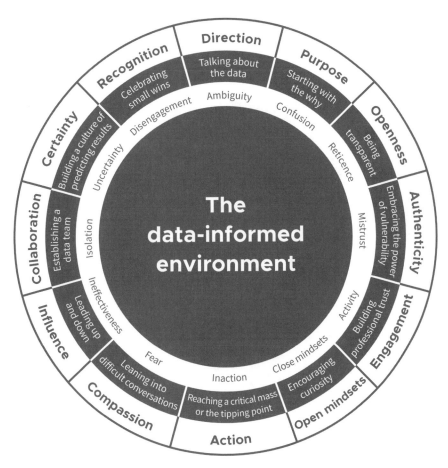

Figure E.1: Completed wheel of factors required to prime the environment.

change process with conditions that are conducive to effective school improvement and that are required to maximize the chance of success.

Change is never easy, and so many significant change efforts fail, but when you carefully plan your approach, reflect on and build your own leadership style, build a team of people around you who are aligned with the vision, and seek to learn with and for your team, you set yourself up for success. Never forget that the reason you became a leader in the first place was to enact positive change and lead great outcomes for the students in your care. They are relying on you to be the best leader you can be so that you inspire change in the school and in their classrooms. Greater outcomes mean better life chances for our students—don't ever underestimate the power that you have as a compassionate and effective data-informed leader. Good luck, and enjoy the challenge!

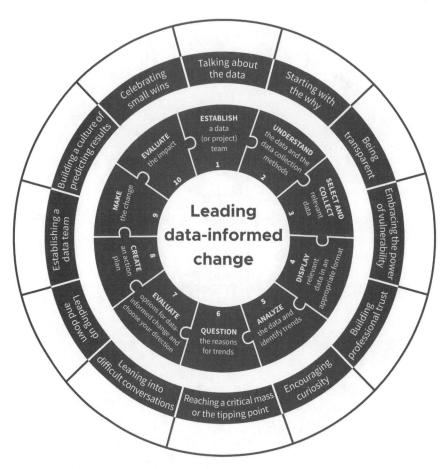

Figure E.2: The change process in the primed environment.

APPENDIX

Template 1: Exploring and Analyzing Different Types of Data

This template can be used to consider data for a cohort, class, or learning area.

Group:			Focus area:		

Assessment 1

% of students below average	% of students at the average	% of students above average

Assessment 2

% of students below average	% of students at the average	% of students above average

Assessment 3

% of students below average	% of students at the average	% of students above average

Things I notice about the data:

Things I wonder about the data:

Questions I have about the data:

Specific steps for modifying teaching/programs/approaches:

Leading Data-Informed Change in Schools © 2021 Solution Tree Press and Hawker Brownlow Education
SolutionTree.com • Visit **go.SolutionTree.com/leadership** to download this free reproducible.

Group: Grade 3 Students			Focus area: Literacy (Reading)		

Assessment 1: Standardized test in reading comprehension			Assessment 2: External assessment in reading		
% of students below average	% of students at the average	% of students above average	% of students below average	% of students at the average	% of students above average
1/9 = 11%	3/9 = 33%	5/9 = 56%	5/9 = 56%	2/9 = 22%	2/9 = 22%

Assessment 3: English learning area result		
% of students below average	% of students at the average	% of students above average
4/9 = 44%	4/9 = 44%	1/9 = 11%

Things I notice about the data:

- There is quite a different spread between the standardized assessment in reading comprehension (mid-high) and external assessment/learning area data (mid-low).
- The learning area data spread is similar to the external assessment results (low-mid).
- Some students have similar results across learning areas (that is, Markus), but others have quite varied learning area results (that is, Caitlin).
- Some students have learning area data that align with their standardized and external results (that is, Bobby) and some that are quite different (that is, Mike).

Leading Data-Informed Change in Schools © 2021 Solution Tree Press and Hawker Brownlow Education
SolutionTree.com • Visit **go.SolutionTree.com/leadership** to download this free reproducible.

Things I wonder about the data:	Questions I have about the data:
• I wonder why students performed so differently in the standardized assessment compared with the external assessment. • I wonder what genre the assessment result is for English (and whether this aligns with the genre of writing in the test). • I am interested in learning more about the literacy demands of mathematics and science. How relevant is reading comprehension?	• What led to the significant improvement in the standardized assessment data? • When was each set of data collected? • Given that the standardized and external assessments are in reading comprehension only, and English is more than comprehension alone, is it fair to assume that students are more likely mid-low?

Specific steps for modifying teaching/programs/approaches:
- Break down specific areas of the standardized and external results to see the differences in the strands that were assessed. Are they all very different, or are some similar? If they are similar, then how can a program be adjusted to cater for this area of weakness?
- Find out the role that reading comprehension plays in mathematics and science and see whether these teachers can embed more explicit reading comprehension strategies in their teaching.
- Consider the English results and the structure/scaffolding required for the next task to help build the skills needed for the students to pass the learning area. Put strategies in place to make these adjustments ASAP.
- Differentiate support for different students (for example, Bobby has needs that are very different from Markus's).

This represents a completed example of Template 1.

Template 2: Exploratory Analysis

This template could be used for exploring the data for a cohort, class, or learning area analysis.

Guiding questions	Response
What is the particular area of interest?	
What trends do you immediately notice in the data?	
Identify three areas of strength in the data.	1. 2. 3.
What does each of the strengths tell you about your programs, strategies, or teaching and learning?	1. 2. 3.
How can you celebrate the areas of strength?	1. 2. 3.
Identify three areas of concern in the data.	1. 2. 3.
What does each of the areas of concern tell you about your programs, strategies, or teaching and learning?	1. 2. 3.
How can you address or make changes to improve the areas of concern?	1. 2. 3.

Guiding questions	Response
What is the particular area of interest?	Grade 3 students' literacy, specifically reading comprehension
What trends do you immediately notice in the data?	• There is quite a different spread between standardized testing (mid-high) and external testing/learning area data (mid-low). • The learning area data spread is similar to the external testing results (low-mid). • Some students have similar results across learning areas (that is, Markus), but others have quite varied learning area results (that is, Caitlin). • Some students have learning area data that align with their standardized and external results (that is, Bobby) and some that are quite different (that is, Mike).
Identify three areas of strength in the data.	1. Standardized testing in reading comprehension results—more than half the students are above average. 2. Science results—the overall results in this learning area are generally higher than English and mathematics. 3. Markus's results across standardized testing and learning area results are very good.
What does each of the strengths tell you about your programs, strategies, or teaching and learning?	1. Students have good reading comprehension skills—it's not possible to fluke such good results in standardized testing. 2. The science program is obviously going well. Students are achieving well in this learning area. 3. Markus is a high-performing student who seems to be given the opportunity to be extended.
How can you celebrate the areas of strength?	1. Share the achievement of the group with students, in a newsletter, with staff, or at an assembly. See whether much progress has been made from the previous standardized test and celebrate progress too where appropriate. 2. Recognize the achievement of the science department—congratulate the head of the learning area and teachers for their pleasing results. Learn from these teachers about what is working well in science to see whether it is transferable to other learning areas. 3. Share Markus's achievements with his class, teachers, parents, and Markus himself.

Leading Data-Informed Change in Schools © 2021 Solution Tree Press and Hawker Brownlow Education
SolutionTree.com • Visit **go.SolutionTree.com/leadership** to download this free reproducible.

Identify three areas of concern in the data.	1. External reading tests—more than half the students are at or below the national minimum standard. 2. English results—nearly half the students failed the learning area. 3. Bobby's results—his results across standardized testing and learning areas are low.
What does each of the areas of concern tell you about your programs, strategies, or teaching and learning?	1. Students' reading comprehension skills were not demonstrated in this assessment—very different results to standardized testing. 2. Students have not performed as well in English as they did in mathematics and science. 3. Bobby is probably not able to adequately access the curriculum as his literacy levels are low.
How can you address or make changes to improve the areas of concern?	1. More information is required to consider the validity of external versus standardized tests. Which seems to be a more accurate reflection of the students' abilities? Do they have strengths or weaknesses in any similar areas across tests? If so, what changes can be made to address these challenges? 2. It raises questions as to what is happening in English— was the genre particularly difficult, was the teaching team consistent, did cross-marking/moderation occur, are these results accurate? What can be done to address this challenge? 3. Reflect on the differentiation strategies in place for Bobby. Could he use additional support staff assistance? Is behavior a factor? If so, is there somewhere that he should be positioned in the room to maximize progress? Are adequate structures/scaffolding in place for Bobby? Is a disrupted home life/illness/other extenuating circumstance affecting his performance? Put new strategies in place that you believe could help Bobby.

This represents a completed example of Template 2.

Leading Data-Informed Change in Schools © 2021 Solution Tree Press and Hawker Brownlow Education
SolutionTree.com • Visit **go.SolutionTree.com/leadership** to download this free reproducible.

Template 3: Bright Spots

This template could be used to identify good news stories in a cohort, class, or learning area analysis.

Guiding questions	Response
What is the particular focus area?	
What positive trends are immediately identifiable in the data?	
What are three bright spots in the data?	1. 2. 3.
Why is each of these things a bright spot?	1. 2. 3.
What element of your school program or approaches has led to the bright spots?	1. 2. 3.
How can you celebrate these bright spots?	1. 2. 3.
What learning is there from these bright spots for other areas of the school?	1. 2. 3.

page 1 of 3

Guiding questions	Response
What is the particular focus area?	Grade 3 students' literacy, specifically reading comprehension
What positive trends are immediately identifiable in the data?	• There is quite a different spread between standardized testing (mid-high) and external testing/learning area data (mid-low). • The learning area data spread is similar to the external testing results (low-mid). • Some students have similar results across learning areas (that is, Markus), but others have quite varied learning area results (that is, Caitlin). • Some students have learning area data that align with their standardized and external results (that is, Bobby) and some that are quite different (that is, Mike).
What are three bright spots in the data?	1. Standardized test in reading comprehension results—more than half the students are above average. 2. Science results—the overall results in this learning area are generally higher than English and mathematics. 3. Markus's results across standardized testing and learning area results are very good.
Why is each of these things a bright spot?	1. Reading comprehension is an important skill for all students to develop. Standardized testing is a reliable measure of students' reading comprehension skills. 2. This learning area is outperforming other learning areas. It is good to see success in science—hopefully these results reflect good engagement and effort on the students' behalf. It is also a reflection of the skills of the science department—they are getting better results out of students than other departments. 3. Markus will be pleased to see his results, and it is good that he is able to achieve results commensurate with his ability.
What element of your school program or approaches has led to the bright spots?	1. Students have good reading comprehension skills—it's not possible to fluke such good results in standardized testing. 2. The science program is obviously going well. Students are achieving well in this learning area. 3. Markus is a high-performing student who seems to be given the opportunity to be extended.

page 2 of 3

Leading Data-Informed Change in Schools © 2021 Solution Tree Press and Hawker Brownlow Education
SolutionTree.com • Visit **go.SolutionTree.com/leadership** to download this free reproducible.

How can you celebrate these bright spots?	1. Share the achievement of the group with students/in a newsletter/with staff/at an assembly. See whether much progress has been made from the previous standardized test and celebrate progress too, where appropriate. 2. Recognize the achievement of the science department—congratulate the head of the learning area and teachers for their pleasing results. 3. Share Markus's achievements with his class, teachers, parents, and Markus himself.
What learning is there from these bright spots for other areas of the school?	1. Look at the areas of strength in the standardized test in reading comprehension. Consider why a particular strand has a higher success rate—what is happening in the current curriculum for this to occur? Assuming that there is one strand lower than the others, how can we translate this information into practice? How do we explicitly teach the skills the students need? 2. Learn from these teachers about what is working well in science to see whether it is transferable to other learning areas. See whether teachers are explicitly teaching science vocabulary, reading text, or doing reading comprehension activities—see what could be picked up by other learning areas. 3. Students have the potential to achieve excellent results in this school, and it is important that activities are differentiated across learning areas to ensure that students of all ability levels are being challenged.

This represents a completed example of Template 3.

Leading Data-Informed Change in Schools © 2021 Solution Tree Press and Hawker Brownlow Education
SolutionTree.com • Visit **go.SolutionTree.com/leadership** to download this free reproducible.

Template 4: Intervention or Areas of Concern

Guiding questions	Response
What is the particular focus area?	
What are the immediately identifiable trends in the data?	
What are the three most significant areas of concern? (List from most pressing to least pressing.)	1. 2. 3.
Why is each of these areas concerning?	1. 2. 3.
What does each of these areas of concern tell you about your programs, strategies, or learning and teaching?	1. 2. 3.
How can you address each of the areas of concern (what changes, strategies, or approaches could you use to address these concerns)?	1. 2. 3.
Do these areas of weakness impact or reflect any other areas of your school programs or approaches?	1. 2. 3.

page 1 of 3

Guiding questions	Response
What is the particular focus area?	Grade 3 students' literacy, specifically reading comprehension
What are the immediately identifiable trends in the data?	• There is quite a different spread between standardized testing (mid-high) and external testing/learning area data (mid-low). • The learning area data spread is similar to the external results (low-mid). • Some students have similar results across learning areas (that is, Markus), but others have quite varied learning area results (that is, Caitlin). • Some students have learning area data that align with their standardized/external testing results (that is, Bobby) and some that are quite different (that is, Mike).
What are the three most significant areas of concern? (List from most pressing to least pressing.)	1. External reading testing—more than half the students are at or below the national minimum standard. 2. English results—nearly half the students failed the learning area. 3. Bobby's results—his results across standardized testing and learning areas are low.
Why is each of these areas concerning?	1. Reading is an important skill that all students need so they can effectively engage in society in the future. The school should be working with students to improve their literacy skills as much as possible—particularly when they are below average. 2. Students should be succeeding in English—particularly when they are achieving good results in other learning areas. Is there a problem with the learning area? With the marking? It's important to ascertain details about the issue so it can be addressed. 3. Bobby is a young man who obviously finds literacy difficult. It's important for his engagement in society in the future that he is able to read and write to a level that enables him to gain employment and live and function as a contributing member of society.
What does each of these areas of concern tell you about your programs, strategies, or learning and teaching?	1. Students' reading comprehension skills were not demonstrated in this assessment—very different results to standardized testing. 2. Students have not performed as well in English as they did in mathematics and science. 3. Bobby is probably not able to adequately access the curriculum as his literacy levels are low.

page 2 of 3

How can you address each of the areas of concern (what changes, strategies, or approaches could you use to address these concerns)?	1. More information is required to consider the validity of external vs. standardized tests. Which seems to be a more accurate reflection of the students' abilities? Do they have strengths/weaknesses in any similar areas across tests? 2. It raises questions as to what is happening in English—was the genre particularly difficult, was the teaching team consistent, did cross-marking/moderation occur, are these results accurate? 3. Reflect on the differentiation strategies in place for Bobby. Could he use additional support staff assistance? Is behavior a factor? If so, is there somewhere that he should be positioned in the room to maximize progress? Are adequate structures/scaffolding in place for Bobby? Is a disrupted home life/illness/other extenuating circumstance affecting his performance?
Do these areas of weakness impact or reflect any other areas of your school programs or approaches?	4. Reading comprehension seems to be affecting performance in other learning areas—mathematics teachers report that students struggle with problem solving and deciphering questions, and humanities teachers report students' lack of interest in reading texts. This seems to be a schoolwide problem rather than an issue with a standardized test. 5. It is worth considering what is working in other learning areas, as the English results are much lower. Further analysis is required to ascertain student performance in other learning areas to see whether there are any other trends. 6. Is adequate support/mentoring in place for Bobby? This result could lead to broader conversations across the school about not letting students fall through the cracks.

This represents a completed example of Template 4.

REFERENCES AND RESOURCES

Artificial intelligence: March of the machines. (2016, June 25). *The Economist*. Accessed at www.economist .com/leaders/2016/06/25/march-of-the-machines on September 14, 2020.

Australian Council for Educational Research. (2016). *National School Improvement Tool*. Accessed at https:// research.acer.edu.au/cgi/viewcontent.cgi?article=1019&context=tll_misc on September 14, 2020.

Australian Institute for Teaching and School Leadership. (2011). *Australian Professional Standards for Teachers*. Accessed at www.aitsl.edu.au/docs/default-source/teach-documents/australian -professional-standards-for-teachers.pdf on September 14, 2020.

Australian Institute for Teaching and School Leadership. (2019). *Australian Professional Standards for Principals and the Leadership Profiles*. Accessed at www.aitsl.edu.au/docs/default-source/national -policy-framework/australian-professional-standard-for-principals.pdf?sfvrsn=c07eff3c_4 on September 14, 2020.

Bain, A., & Swan, G. (2011). Technology-enhanced feedback tools as a knowledge management mechanism for supporting professional growth and school reform. *Educational Technology Research and Development*, *59*(5), 673–685. Accessed at https://doi.org/10.1007/s11423–011–9201-x on September 14, 2020.

Barber, M. (2005, September 27). Australia could learn a thing or two from Britain's educational reforms. *The Sydney Morning Herald*. Accessed at https://amp.smh.com.au/national/australia-could-learn -a-thing-or-two-from-britains-educational-reforms-20050927-gdm50j.html on September 14, 2020.

Bernhardt, V. L. (2018). *Data analysis for comprehensive schoolwide improvement (4th ed.)*. New York, NY: Routledge.

Bill and Melinda Gates Foundation. (2015). *Teachers know best: Making data work for teachers and students*. Accessed at http://k12education.gatesfoundation.org/download/?Num=2335&filename=Teachers KnowBest-MakingDataWork.compressed.pdf on September 14, 2020.

Bocala, C. (2013, January 31). *TeachingWorks January seminar: Using data to inform instruction* [PowerPoint slides]. Accessed at www.teachingworks.org/images/files/TeachingWorks_Data_Wise_013013_no _pictures.pdf on September 14, 2020.

Boudett, K. P., & City, E. A. (2013). Lessons from the Data Wise Project: Three habits of mind for building a collaborative culture. *Harvard Education Letter*, *29*(3). Accessed at www.hepg.org/hel-home /issues/29_3/helarticle/lessons-from-the-data-wise-project_567 on September 14, 2020.

Boudett, K. P., City, E. A., & Murnane, R. J. (Eds.). (2013). *Data wise: A step-by-step guide to using assessment results to improve teaching and learning* (Revised and expanded ed.). Cambridge, MA: Harvard Education Press.

British Columbia Teachers' Council. (2019). *Professional standards for BC educators*. Accessed at www2 .gov.bc.ca/assets/gov/education/kindergarten-to-grade-12/teach/teacher-regulation/standards-for -educators/edu_standards.pdf on September 14, 2020.

Brown, B. (2010, June). *The power of vulnerability* [Video file]. Accessed at www.ted.com/talks/brene_brown _on_vulnerability on September 14, 2020.

Brown, B. (2015a). *Daring greatly: How the courage to be vulnerable transforms the way we live, love, parent, and lead*. London: Penguin Life.

Brown, B. (2015b). *Rising strong: How the ability to reset transforms the way we live, love, parent, and lead*. New York: Random House.

Brown, B. (2018). *Dare to lead: Brave work, tough conversations, whole hearts*. New York: Random House.

Brown, B. (2019). *Super Soul sessions: The anatomy of trust* [Video file]. Accessed at https://brenebrown .com/videos/anatomy-trust-video/ on September 14, 2020.

Burke, W. W., & Litwin, G. H. (1992). A causal model of organizational performance and change. *Journal of Management*, *18*(3), 523–545. Accessed at https://doi.org/10.1177/014920639201800306 on September 14, 2020.

Call, K. (2018). Professional teaching standards: A comparative analysis of their history, implementation and efficacy. *Australian Journal of Teacher Education*, *43*(3), 93–108. Accessed at http://dx.doi .org/10.14221/ajte.2018v43n3.6 on September 14, 2020.

Coach4Growth. (n.d.). *High low matrix coaching model: Coaching techniques for will and skill issues*. Accessed at https://coach4growth.com/coaching-skills/high-low-matrix-coaching-model-coaching-techniques -for-will-and-skill-issues on September 14, 2020.

Corwin. (2019, July 31). *Fisher, Frey & Almarode PLC+: The plus is YOU* [Video file]. Accessed at www.youtube .com/watch?v=Q6_WrcQ2vFI on September 14, 2020.

Data is giving rise to a new economy. (2017, May 6). *The Economist*. Accessed at www.economist.com /briefing/2017/05/06/data-is-giving-rise-to-a-new-economy on September 14, 2020.

Deal, T. E., & Kennedy, A. A. (1982). *Corporate cultures: The rites and rituals of corporate life*. Boston: Addison-Wesley.

Dewey, J. (1963). *Experience and education*. New York: Collier Books.

Duffy, F. M. (2008). Strategic communication during times of great change. *School Administrator*, *65*(4), 24–28.

Duffy, F. M., & Reigeluth, C. M. (2008). The School System Transformation (SST) protocol. *Educational Technology*, *48*(4), 41–49.

DuFour, R., DuFour, R., Eaker, R., Many, T. W., & Mattos, M. (2017). *Learning by doing: A handbook for Professional Learning Communities at Work* (Rev. 3rd ed.). Cheltenham, Victoria, Australia: Hawker Brownlow Education.

Dweck, C. S. (2008). *Mindset: The new psychology of success*. New York: Random House.

Evidence for Learning. (2019). *Putting evidence to work: A school's guide to implementation*. Accessed at https://evidenceforlearning.org.au/assets/Guidance-Reports/Implementation/Guidance-Report -Putting-evidence-to-work-a-schools-guide-to-implementation.pdf on September 14, 2020.

Ezard, T. (2015). *The buzz: Creating a thriving and collaborative learning culture*. Melbourne, Victoria, Australia: Author.

Fisher, J., & Good, J. (2019, September 10). *AI in action: Reshaping analytics* [Video file]. Accessed at www .brighttalk.com/webcast/15749/368888/ai-in-action-reshaping-analytics on September 14, 2020.

Fleming, R., Pringle, T., Barker, T., Fisher, J., & Potter, D. (2019, August 15). *Make your data dance: Qlik virtual forum talkshow* [Video file]. Accessed at www.brighttalk.com/webcast/15749/366561/make-your-data -dance-qlik-virtual-forum-talkshow on September 14, 2020.

Frei, F. (2018, April). *How to build (and rebuild) trust* [Video file]. Accessed at www.ted.com/talks/frances_frei _how_to_build_and_rebuild_trust on September 14, 2020.

Gladwell, M. (2006). *The tipping point: How little things can make a big difference*. New York: Little, Brown.

Goldrick, L. (2002). *Improving teacher evaluation to improve teaching quality*. Washington, DC: National Governors Association Center for Best Practices. Accessed at https://files.eric.ed.gov/fulltext /ED480159.pdf on September 14, 2020.

Gupta, G., & Rosenfeldt, R. (2018). *The case for change leadership in development projects*. Accessed at www.kotterinc.com/wp-content/uploads/2019/10/The-Case-for-Change-Leadership-in-Development -Projects.pdf on September 14, 2020.

Harari, Y. N. (2016). *Homo deus: A brief history of tomorrow*. New York: Random House.

Harvard Graduate School of Education. (n.d.). *About Data Wise*. Accessed at https://datawise.gse.harvard .edu/about on September 14, 2020.

Hattie, J. (2008). *Visible learning: A synthesis of over 800 meta-analyses relating to achievement*. New York: Routledge.

Holbeche, L. (2006). *Understanding change: Theory, implementation and success*. Oxford, England: Butterworth-Heinemann.

Houchins, D. E., Gagnon, J. C., Lane, H. B., Lambert, R. G., & McCray, E. D. (2018). The efficacy of a literacy intervention for incarcerated adolescents. *Residential Treatment for Children & Youth*, *35*(1), 60–91. Accessed at https://doi.org/10.1080/0886571X.2018.1448739 on September 14, 2020.

Hunter + Geist, Inc. (2011). *Lobato v. the State of Colorado: Trial day 21*. Accessed at https://static1 .squarespace.com/static/55688532e4b0e4f916bef849/5568857ce4b00fceede109f5/5568857 ce4b00fceede10ab2/1374703821287/Lobato-Trial-Day-21.pdf on September 14, 2020.

Hutton, T. (2017, May 15). *Teachers are sick of the big D: Teaching in the age of big D*. Accessed at www .mrhutton.com/teachers-sick-big-d/ on September 14, 2020.

Ingvarson, L., Elliott, A., Kleinhenz, E., & McKenzie, P. (2006). *Teacher education accreditation: A review of national and international trends and practices*. Camberwell, Victoria, Australia: Australian Council for Educational Research. Accessed at https://research.acer.edu.au/cgi/viewcontent.cgi ?article=1000&context=teacher_education on September 14, 2020.

International Association for the Evaluation of Educational Achievement. (2019a). *PIRLS: Progress in International Reading Literacy Study*. Accessed at www.iea.nl/studies/iea/pirls on September 14, 2020.

International Association for the Evaluation of Educational Achievement. (2019b). *TIMSS: Trends in International Mathematics and Science Study*. Accessed at www.iea.nl/studies/iea/timss on September 14, 2020.

Jackson, D., & Jackson, J. (2018). *How to speak human: A practical guide to getting the best from the humans you work with*. Milton, Queensland, Australia: John Wiley & Sons Australia.

Jobs, S. (2011). *Steve Jobs: His own words and wisdom*. Cupertino, CA: Silicon Valley Press.

Jones, S., & Pickett, M. (2019). *Making the data-driven journey easy* [Video file]. Accessed at www.brighttalk .com/webcast/15971/364868 on September 14, 2020.

Junio, E., Plumlee, D., Patil, N., & Shah, T. (2019, June 12). *Data visualisation and the power of storytelling* [Video file]. Accessed at www.brighttalk.com/webcast/17596/359358 on September 14, 2020.

Kahneman, D. (2011). *Thinking, fast and slow*. New York: Farrar, Straus and Giroux.

Knapp, M. S., Swinnerton, J. A., Copland, M. A., & Monpas-Huber, J. (2006). *Data-informed leadership in education*. Seattle, WA: Center for the Study of Teaching and Policy.

Knight, J. (2016). *Better conversations: Coaching ourselves and each other to be more credible, caring, and connected*. Thousand Oaks, CA: Corwin Press.

Koji, D. (2016, December 8). *An inspiring discussion with Simon Sinek about learning your "why."* Accessed at www.entrepreneur.com/article/284791 on September 14, 2020.

Kotter, J. P. (n.d.). *8-step process*. Accessed at www.kotterinc.com/8-steps-process-for-leading-change/ on September 14, 2020.

Kotter, J. P. (1995). Leading change: Why transformation efforts fail. *Harvard Business Review*, *73*(3), 59–67.

Kotter, J. P. (1996). *Leading change*. Cambridge, MA: Harvard Business Review Press.

Kotter, J. P. (2017). *The problem with data*. Accessed at www.kotterinc.com/wp-content/uploads/2017/11 /The-Problem-With-Data-Kotter-2017.pdf on September 14, 2020.

Landsberg, M. (2003). *The tao of coaching: Boost your effectiveness at work by inspiring and developing those around you*. London: Profile Books.

Lencioni, P. (2002). *The five dysfunctions of a team: A leadership fable*. Hoboken, NJ: John Wiley & Sons.

Loewenstein, G. (1994). The psychology of curiosity: A review and reinterpretation. *Psychological Bulletin*, *116*(1), 75–98.

Mackinlay, J., Kosara, R., & Wallace, M. (2013). *Data storytelling: Using visualization to share the human impact of numbers*. Seattle, WA: Tableau Software. Accessed at www.tableau.com/sites/default/files /media/whitepaper_datastorytelling.pdf on September 14, 2020.

Marzano, R. J. (2003). *What works in schools: Translating research into action*. Alexandria, VA: Association for Supervision and Curriculum Development.

Matters, G. (2006). *Using data to support learning in schools: Students, teachers, systems*. Camberwell, Victoria, Australia: Australian Council for Educational Research. Accessed at https://research.acer .edu.au/cgi/viewcontent.cgi?article=1004&context=aer on September 14, 2020.

McGeorge, D. (2018). *The 25 minute meeting: Half the time, double the impact*. Milton, Queensland, Australia: John Wiley & Sons Australia.

Ministry of Education. (1997). *Teaching quality standard applicable to the provision of basic education in Alberta*. Accessed at https://education.alberta.ca/media/1626523/english-tqs-card-2013_3.pdf on September 14, 2020.

Mockler, N., & Stacey, M. (2019, March 18). What's good "evidence-based" practice for classrooms? We asked the teachers, here's what they said. *EduResearch Matters*. Accessed at www.aare.edu.au/blog/?p=3844 on September 14, 2020.

National Board for Professional Teaching Standards. (2016). *What teachers should know and be able to do*. Accessed at http://accomplishedteacher.org/wp-content/uploads/2016/12/NBPTS-What-Teachers -Should-Know-and-Be-Able-to-Do-.pdf on September 14, 2020.

National Board for Professional Teaching Standards. (2019). *National Board standards*. Accessed at www .nbpts.org/standards-five-core-propositions/ on September 14, 2020.

National Conference of State Legislatures. (2011). *National Board for Professional Teaching Standards certification: What legislators need to know*. Accessed at www.ncsl.org/Portals/1/Documents/educ /NationalBoard.pdf on September 14, 2020.

North Atlantic Treaty Organization. (2002, June 6). *Press conference by US Secretary of Defence, Donald Rumsfeld*. Accessed at www.nato.int/docu/speech/2002/s020606g.htm on September 14, 2020.

Nova Scotia Department of Education and Early Childhood Development. (2018). *Nova Scotia teaching standards: Excellence in teaching and learning—Comprehensive guide*. Accessed at https://srce.ca /sites/default/files//Nova%20Scotia%20Teaching%20Standards-Comprehensive%20Guide-2018.pdf on September 14, 2020.

Nussbaumer, A., & Merkley, W. (2010). The path of transformational change. *Library Management, 31*(8/9), 678–689. Accessed at https://doi.org/10.1108/01435121011093441 on September 14, 2020.

Oberman, M. E., & Boudett, K. P. (2015). Eight steps to becoming data wise. *Educational Leadership, 73*(3). Accessed at www.ascd.org/publications/educational-leadership/nov15/vol73/num03/Eight-Steps-to -Becoming-Data-Wise.aspx on September 14, 2020.

Oliver, P., Marwell, G., & Teixeira, R. (1985). A theory of the critical mass. I. Interdependence, group heterogeneity, and the production of collective action. *American Journal of Sociology, 91*(3), 522–556. Accessed at https://doi.org/10.1086/228313 on September 14, 2020.

Ontario College of Teachers. (n.d.). *The standards of practice for the teaching profession*. Accessed at www .oct.ca/-/media/PDF/Standards%20Poster/standards_flyer_e.pdf on September 14, 2020.

Organisation for Economic Co-operation and Development. (2018). *Programme for International Student Assessment*. Accessed at www.oecd.org/pisa/ on September 14, 2020.

Pink, D. H. (2011). *Drive: The surprising truth about what motivates us*. New York: Penguin.

Pringle, T. (2019, July 30). *Building a platform for analytics means empowering your people with data* [Video file]. Accessed at www.brighttalk.com/webcast/15749/367156/building-a-platform-for-analytics -means-empowering-your-people-with-data on September 14, 2020.

Reeves, D. B. (2004). *Accountability for learning: How teachers and school leaders can take charge*. Alexandria, VA: Association for Supervision and Curriculum Development.

Rosling, H., Rosling, O., & Rönnlund, A. R. (2018). *Factfulness: Ten reasons we're wrong about the world—and why things are better than you think*. New York: St. Martin's Press.

Scheerens, J. (2002). School self-evaluation: Origins, definition, approaches, methods and implementation. *School-Based Evaluation: An International Perspective, 8*, 35–69. Accessed at https://doi.org/10.1016 /S1474–7863(02)80006–0 on September 14, 2020.

Schildkamp, K., Lai, M. K., & Earl, L. (Eds.). (2013). *Data-based decision making in education: Challenges and opportunities*. New York: Springer.

Schildkamp, K., & Poortman, C. L. (2015). Factors influencing the functioning of data teams. *Teachers College Record*, *117*(4), 1–42.

Schleicher, A. (2012). *Use data to build better schools* [Video file]. Accessed at www.ted.com/talks/andreas _schleicher_use_data_to_build_better_schools on September 14, 2020.

Schleicher, A. (2019, March 29). How Italy developed a state-of-the-art school assessment culture. *OECD Education and Skills Today*. Accessed at https://oecdedutoday.com/italy-national-school-assessment -test-program/ on September 14, 2020.

Schnellert, L. M., Butler, D. L., & Higginson, S. K. (2008). Co-constructors of data, co-constructors of meaning: Teacher professional development in an age of accountability. *Teaching and Teacher Education*, *24*(3), 725–750. Accessed at https://doi.org/10.1016/j.tate.2007.04.001 on September 14, 2020.

Seife, C. (2010). *Proofiness: How you're being fooled by the numbers*. New York: Penguin.

Sharratt, L. (2018). Leading with knowledge in communities of practice. *Australian Educational Leader*, *40*(4), 12–16.

Sharratt, L., & Fullan, M. (2012). *Putting faces on the data: What great leaders do!* Thousand Oaks, CA: Corwin Press.

Shen, J., Cooley, V. E., Ma, X., Reeves, P. L., Burt, W. L., Rainey, J. M., et al. (2012). Data-informed decision making on high-impact strategies: Developing and validating an instrument for principals. *Journal of Experimental Education*, *80*(1), 1–25. Accessed at https://doi.org/10.1080/00220973.2010.550338 on September 14, 2020.

Sinek, S. (2009). *Start with why: How great leaders inspire everyone to take action*. New York: Penguin.

Sinek, S. (2019). *The golden circle presentation* [PowerPoint slides]. Accessed at https://simonsinek.com /commit/the-golden-circle on September 14, 2020.

Singhal, P. (2017, September 27). Australia should take "medical approach to teaching": Expert. *The Sydney Morning Herald*. Accessed at www.smh.com.au/education/australia-should-take-medical-approach -to-teaching-expert-20170927-gypo00.html on September 14, 2020.

Sivers, D. (2010, February 11). *First follower: Leadership lessons from a dancing guy*. Accessed at https:// sivers.org/ff on September 14, 2020.

Swiss, L., Fallon, K. M., & Burgos, G. (2012). Does critical mass matter? Women's political representation and child health in developing countries. *Social Forces*, *91*(2), 531–558. Accessed at https://doi.org/10 .1093/sf/sos169 on September 14, 2020.

Tableau Software. (2019). *Data day out Sydney: On-demand videos* [Video file]. Accessed at www.tableau .com/community/events/virtual-event-data-day-out-sydney-watch#reveal on September 14, 2020.

The Teachers' Council of Thailand. (2018). *Southeast Asia Teachers Competency Framework* (*SEA-TCF*). Accessed at www.criced.tsukuba.ac.jp/math/seameo/2019/pdf/SEA-TCF%20BOOK.pdf on September 14, 2020.

Thomson, A. M., Perry, J. L., & Miller, T. K. (2007). Conceptualizing and measuring collaboration. *Journal of Public Administration Research and Theory*, *19*(1), 23–56. Accessed at https://doi.org/10.1093/jopart /mum036 on September 14, 2020.

United Kingdom Department for Education. (2011). *Teachers' standards: Guidance for school leaders, school staff and governing bodies*. Accessed at https://assets.publishing.service.gov.uk/government/uploads/system/uploads/attachment_data/file/665520/Teachers__Standards.pdf on September 14, 2020.

United Kingdom Department for Education. (2015). *National standards of excellence for headteachers: Departmental advice for headteachers, governing boards and aspiring headteachers*. Accessed at https://assets.publishing.service.gov.uk/government/uploads/system/uploads/attachment_data/file/396247/National_Standards_of_Excellence_for_Headteachers.pdf on September 14, 2020.

Van Damme, D. (2019, April 15). Why knowledge is the most important resource for education systems today. *OECD Education and Skills Today*. Accessed at https://oecdedutoday.com/knowledge-education-policy-research-practice/ on September 14, 2020.

Visible Learning Plus. (2017). *Visible Learning Plus: 250+ influences on student achievement*. Accessed at https://visible-learning.org/wp-content/uploads/2018/03/VLPLUS-252-Influences-Hattie-ranking-DEC-2017.pdf on September 14, 2020.

Wood, D. J., & Gray, B. (1991). Toward a comprehensive theory of collaboration. *Journal of Applied Behavioral Science*, *27*(2), 139–162. Accessed at https://doi.org/10.1177/0021886391272001 on September 14, 2020.

The world's most valuable resource is no longer oil, but data. (2017, May 6). *The Economist*. Accessed at www.economist.com/leaders/2017/05/06/the-worlds-most-valuable-resource-is-no-longer-oil-but-data on September 14, 2020.

INDEX

Got Data? Now What?
Laura Lipton and Bruce Wellman

Complete with survey questions for efficient data collection, group work structures, strategies, and tools—along with essential definitions and descriptions of data types—this compelling guide will help you confront data obstacles and turn struggling committees into powerful communities of learners.
BKF530

Time for Change
Anthony Muhammad and Luis F. Cruz

Exceptional leaders have four distinctive skills: strong communication, the ability to build trust, the ability to increase the skills of those they lead, and a results orientation. *Time for Change* offers powerful guidance for those seeking to develop and strengthen these skills.
BKF683

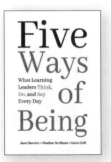

Five Ways of Being
Jane Danvers, Heather De Blasio, and Gavin Grift

In this must-read guide, the authors challenge and reinvent the mindset of leadership. Each chapter outlines one of five ways of being—from forming trusting relationships to being purposeful in thought and action—that will empower you to genuinely lead learning in staff, colleagues, and students.
BKB013

Deep Change Leadership
Douglas Reeves

As 21st century educators grapple with unprecedented challenges, schools and districts require a model of change leadership that responds to shifting environmental realities. In *Deep Change Leadership*, author Douglas Reeves offers up a pragmatic model that embraces engagement, inquiry, and focused action.
BKF935

Solution Tree | Press
a division of

Solution Tree

Visit SolutionTree.com or call 800.733.6786 to order.

Wait! Your professional development journey doesn't have to end with the last pages of this book.

We realize improving student learning doesn't happen overnight. And your school or district shouldn't be left to puzzle out all the details of this process alone.

No matter where you are on the journey, we're committed to helping you get to the next stage.

Take advantage of everything from **custom workshops** to **keynote presentations** and **interactive web and video conferencing**. We can even help you develop an action plan tailored to fit your specific needs.

Let's get the conversation started.

Call 888.763.9045 today.

SolutionTree.com